AF227463

# Eyes Wide Open

*Jon Morgan*

# Contents


Dedication

Acknowledgments

About the Author

After The Fall

Sunrise

The Phoenix

Leviathan

Sunset

Storyteller

Eye of the Storm

Rise

Hemeroscopium

Refinement

Birth of a Mermaid

Ephemeral

Sukha

Dukkha

Blue Man of the Minch

Freed by Forgiveness

Perception

# Dedication

This book is dedicated to my wife and best friend. She is my greatest supporter. The reason I started sculpting, the reason why I want to always be growing and pushing the limits of my potential. Contrary to popular belief, she is not the reference used for my sculpture. Unless that sculpture presents as knock-dead gorgeous, then maybe she had some influence, maybe.

# Acknowledgments

I want to acknowledge the wonderful people who have supported me as I try to create something meaningful. The art world is brutal. Rejection is looking to crush anyone not up to the fight. However, those who have bought my work, those who have taken the time to start a conversation, and those who have simply shown gratitude for the time and effort put into it. You have warmed my heart and fueled my passion to keep going. Thank you

A special thanks to my Editors Ryan Shoemaker, Shawn Zavier and my Photographer Kyle Alstrom-Alexander.

# About the Author

J. Morgan believes that when art is successful, it creates an emotional connection. There is so much good in the world that goes unnoticed. So many people who are a strength to him, so many stories that give him hope and help him be a better person. He tries to embody those stories and ideas through sculpture so that they can be seen and felt by others. He learned early on in his sculpting career that art has the power to make people feel things that are hard to describe. The challenge is to make something interesting enough that they will not only appreciate it visually but realize that there is something more going on with his pieces. Once that happens, a dialogue can begin where awareness and common ground can be explored.

J Morgan wants his art to be more about what it makes someone feel. Sculpture can be a conversation starter, a sculpture that can bring people together, a sculpture that is applicable to our times and our needs. He hopes it can be a conduit to better understanding. If it can make us question what we think we know is true and open our minds to the possibility that there is always more we can learn, then he has accomplished something truly remarkable.

J Morgan's process is all about creating art that connects emotionally with its viewer. He is passionate about finding the good around him, taking those ideas or feelings, and representing them in physical form through bronze sculpture. He avoids references because he doesn't want what is created to avoid personal biases. There are three critical focuses that he uses to define his style. 1. Movement. J Morgan creates incredibly complicated armatures to support unlimited design. This creates added expense to the molding and bronzing process but allows him complete freedom to carry out his ideas. 2. He immediately wants the viewer to realize there is more going on with the sculpture. It has to tell a story. Because the story is integral, he includes it when presenting the sculpture to the public to offer perspective. 3. He also hides things within the sculpture to create layers of what he is trying to say. Something that only someone who takes the time to truly study will find.

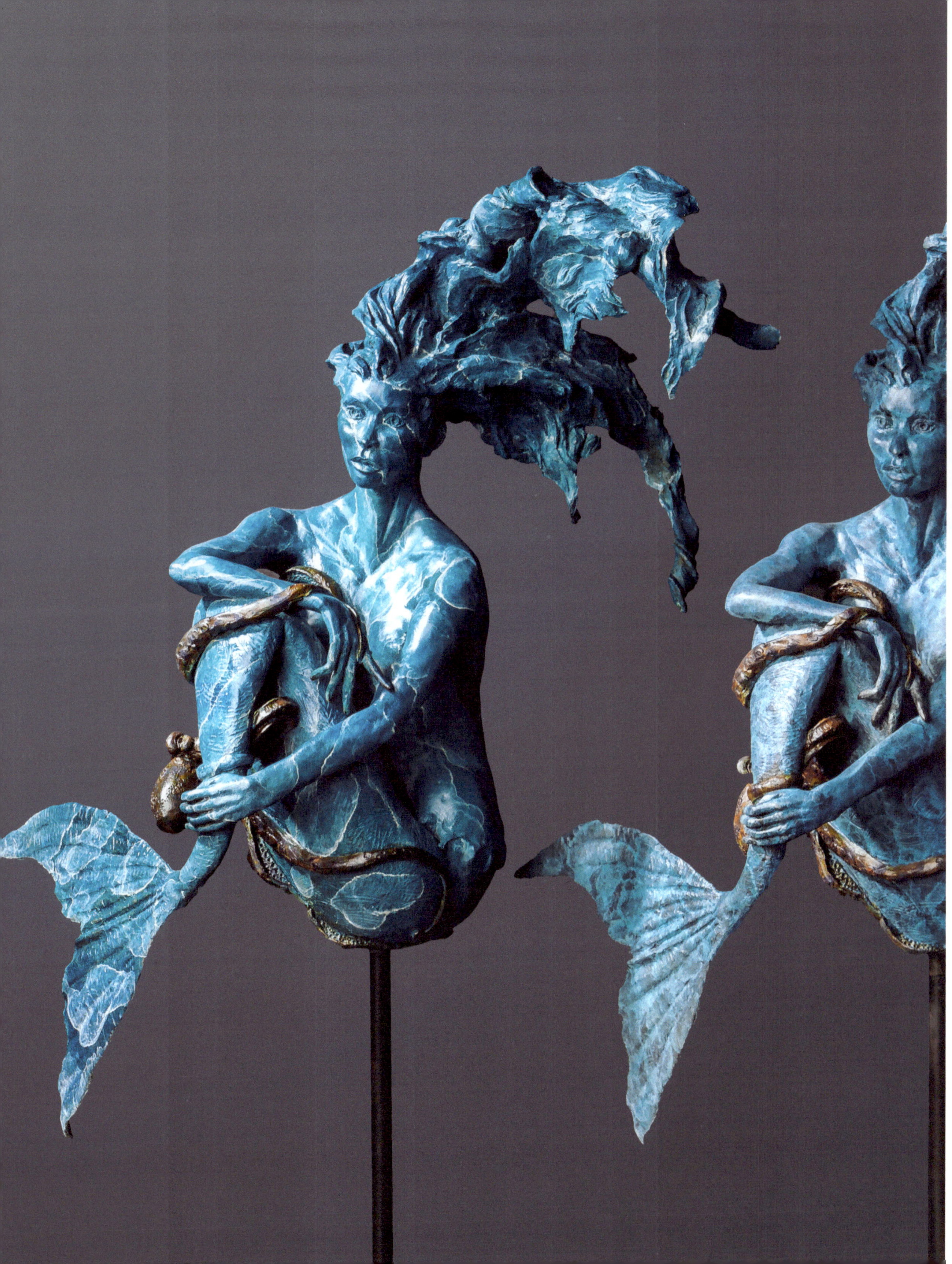

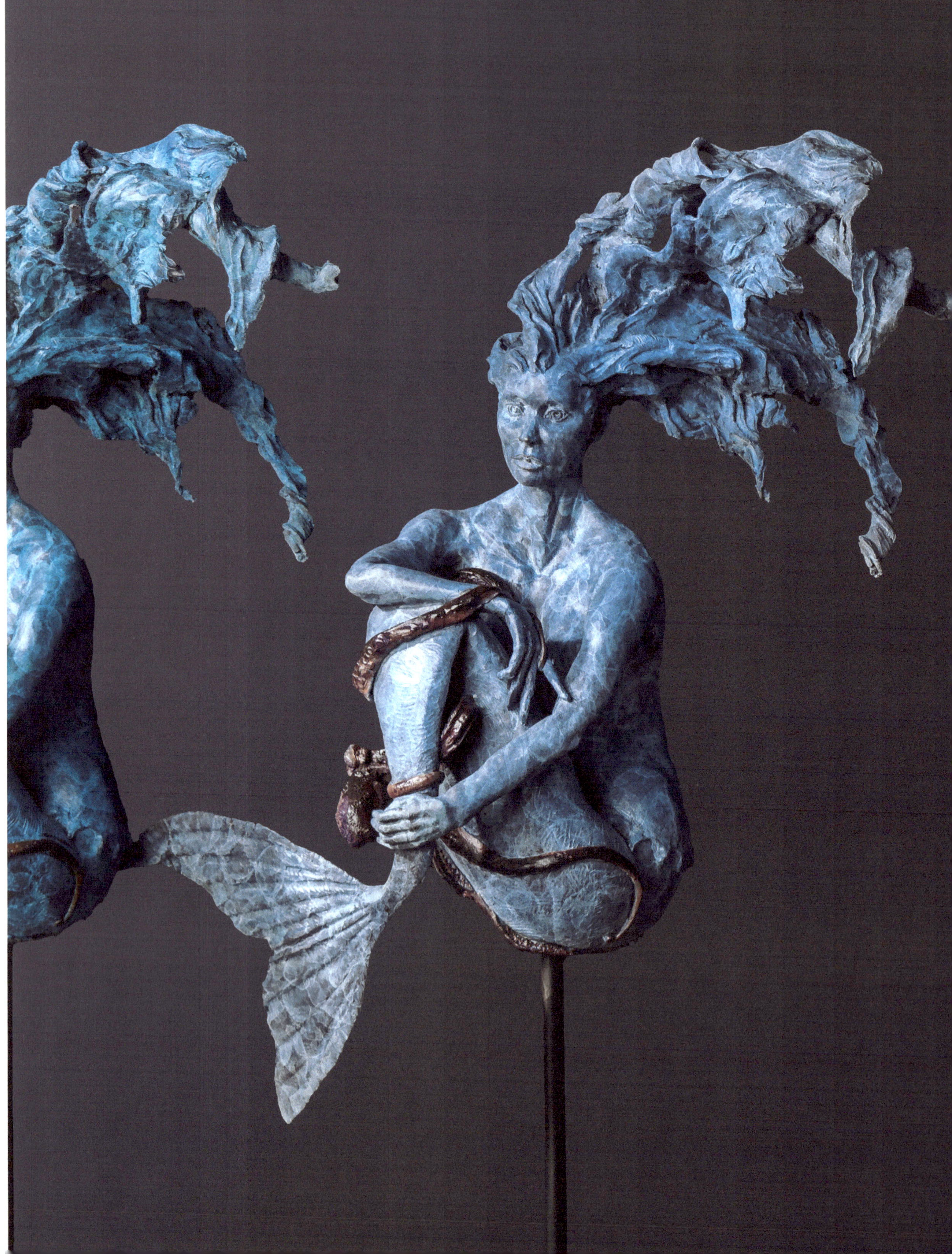

## After The Fall

After the Fall is a tribute to the unconquerable human spirit. What inspired this sculpture was my friendship with a young man paralyzed from the neck down who lived in a long-term care facility where my wife interned. Believing my visits an act of service for him, I soon realized that I was the beneficiary of our time together.

I quickly understood how this amazing young man was not the victim of tragedy; rather, he'd become a conduit of light and joy who'd willingly repurposed his life to lift others instead of wallowing in blame and self-pity. In his joyous presence, I witnessed the embodiment of how our difficulties are really opportunities for growth and learning.

I compare the mythical story of Daedalus and Icarus to all who fall in this life—as we do at times throughout the journey. Daedalus, with his brilliant mind and keen intellect, became an invaluable asset to King Minos, who imprisoned Daedalus and his son Icarus on the island of Crete so they wouldn't fall into enemy hands.

Daedalus, to free himself and his son, constructed wings from feathers and beeswax to fly away from the island. Before their escape, Daedalus warned Icarus not to fly too close to the ocean in case the feathers became wet and not too high in case the sun melted the beeswax. Yet Icarus, thrilled with his new freedom, forgot his father's warning, flew too close to the sun, and plunged to his death.

From time to time in life, all of us fall—but those moments need not define us permanently. I believe that out of these falls emerge moments to find purpose in our struggles. I hope that we embrace our challenges and unite to support and strengthen one another with the unique perspectives and wisdom that adversity brings.

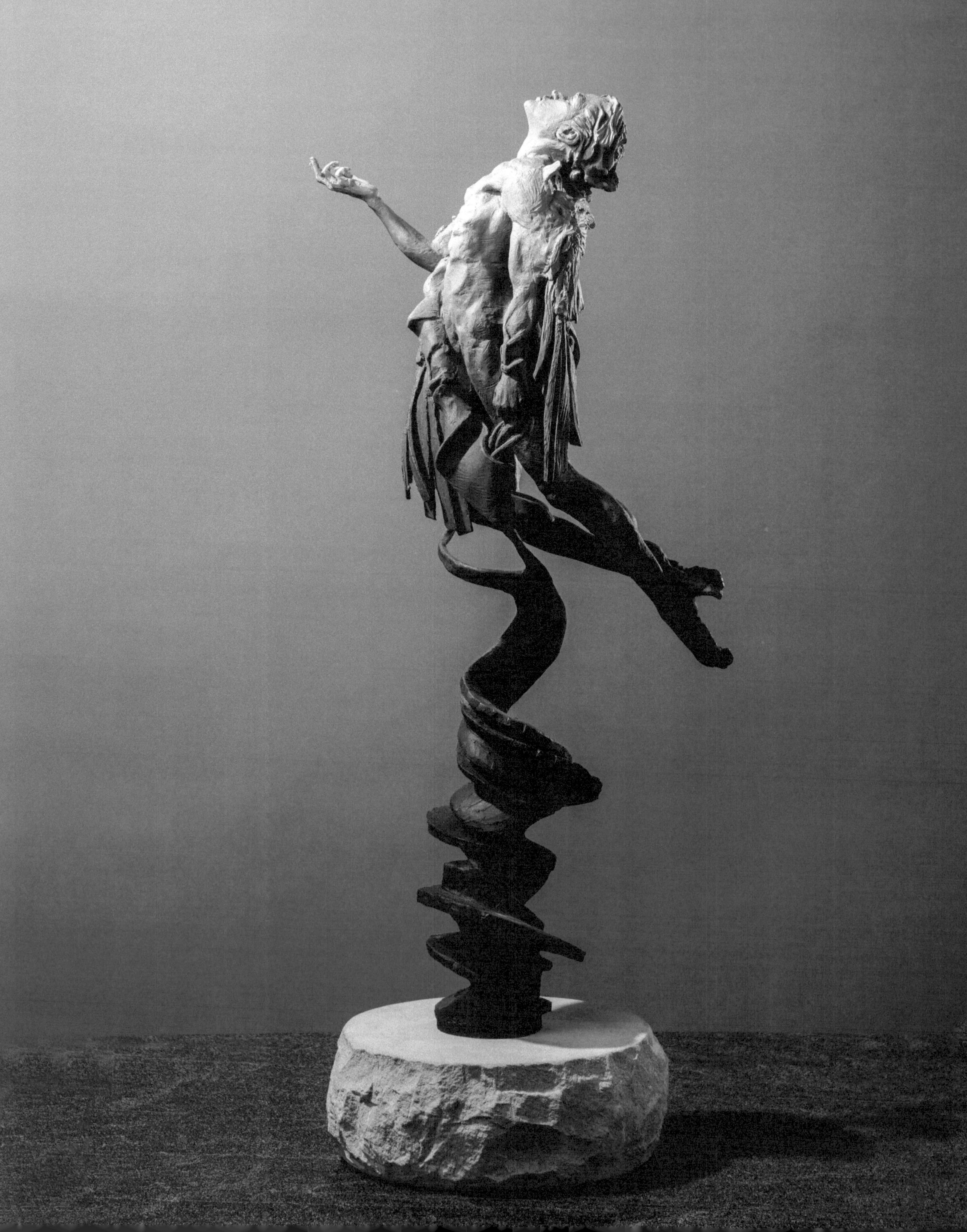

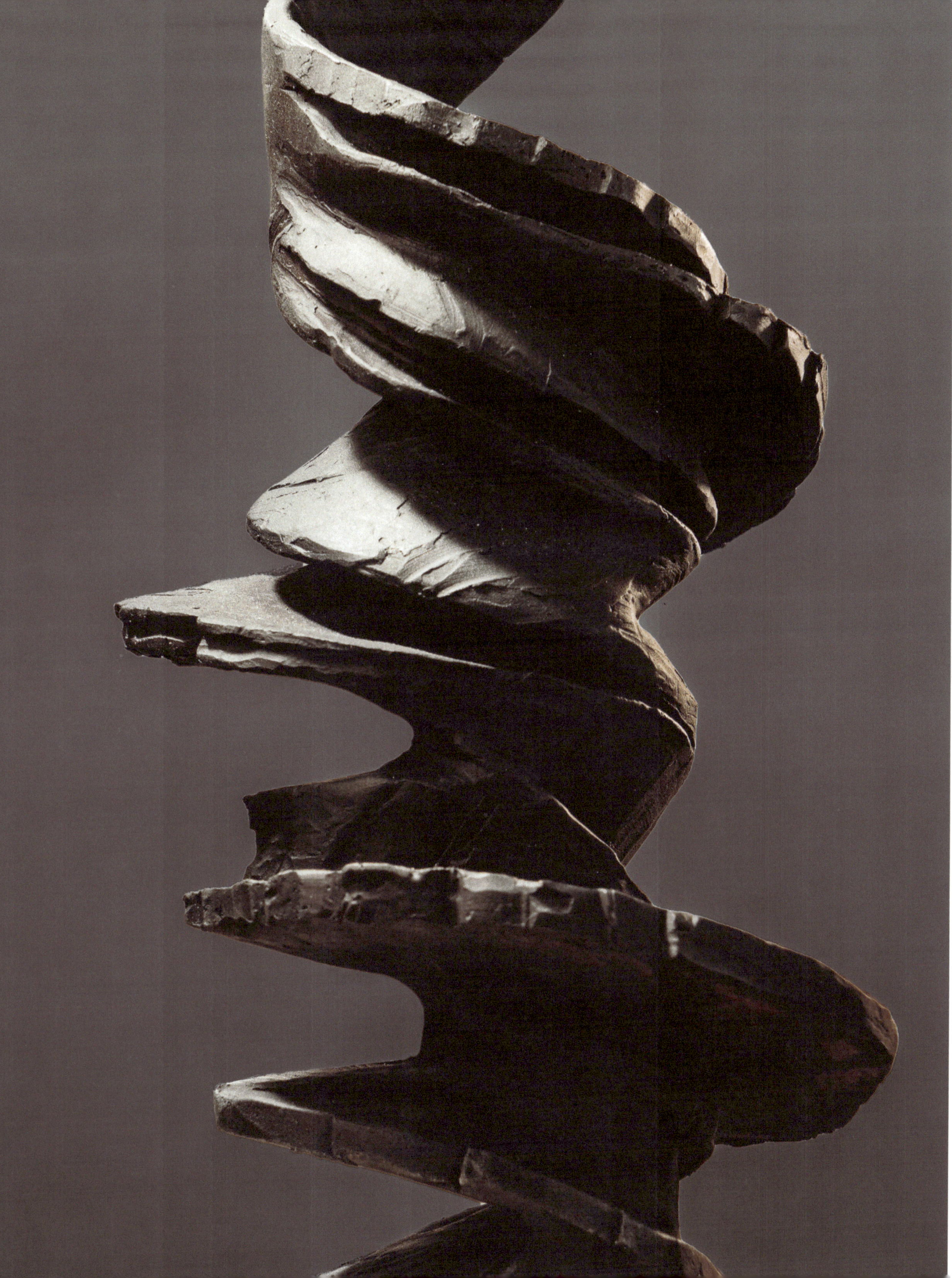

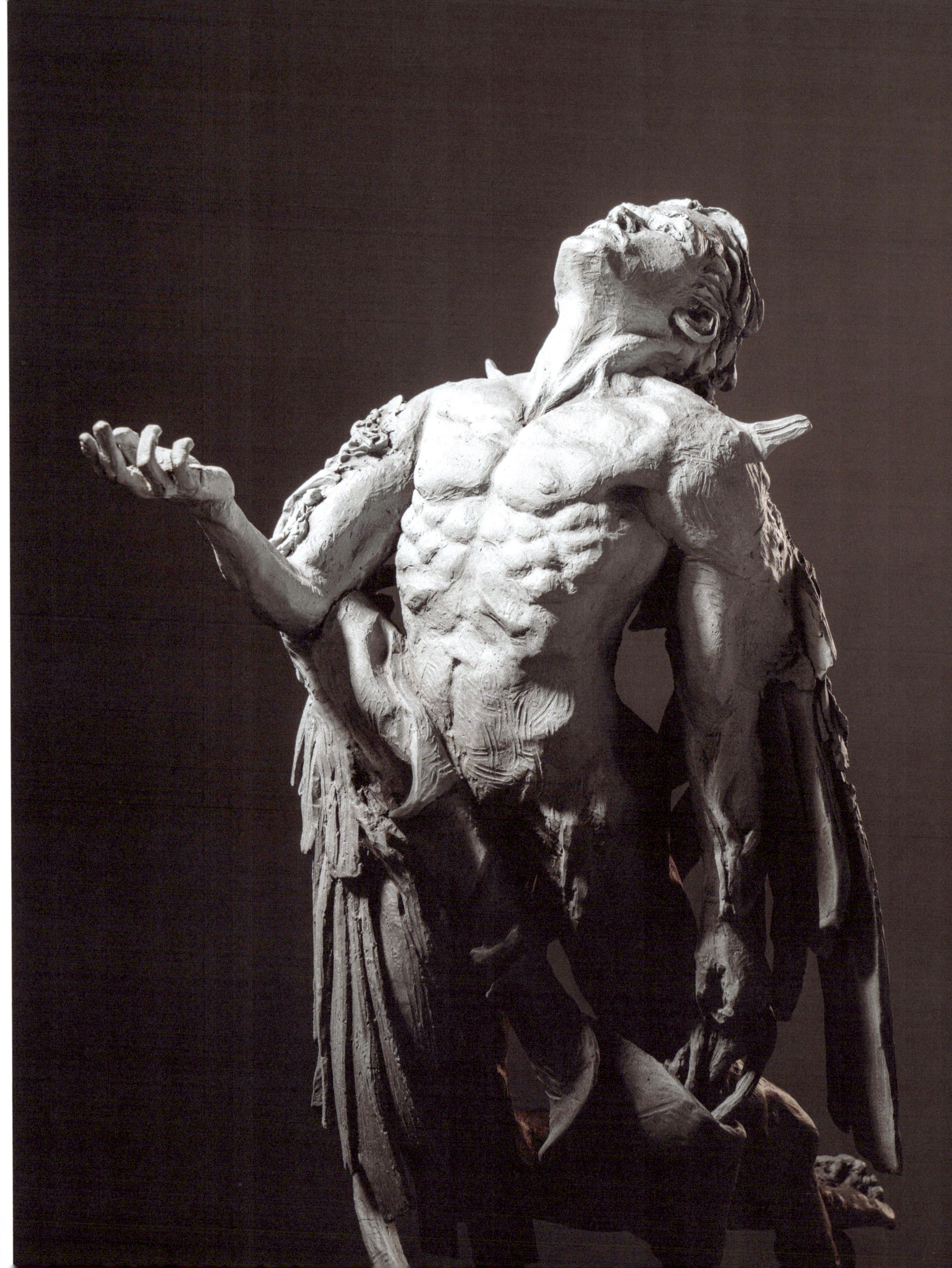

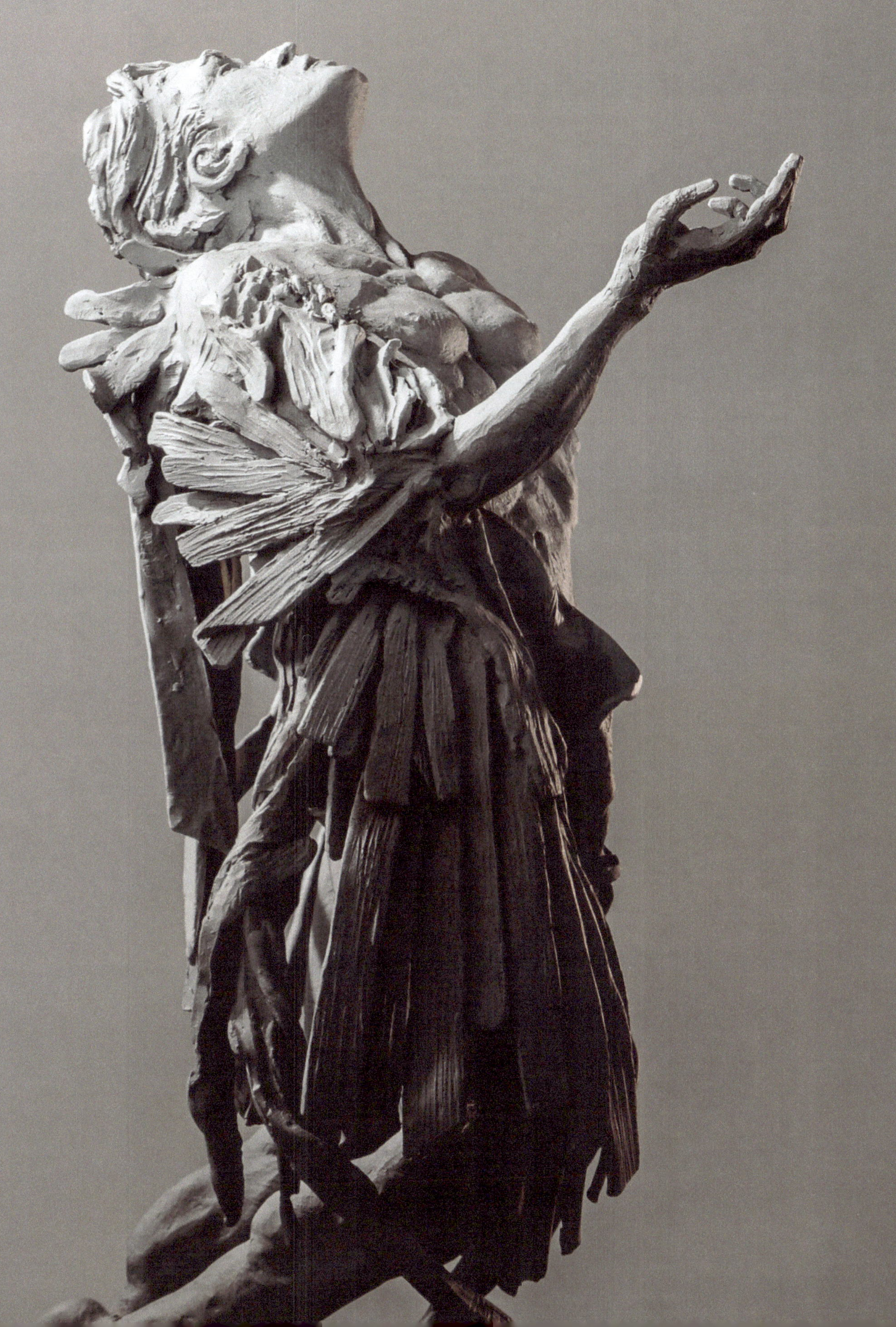

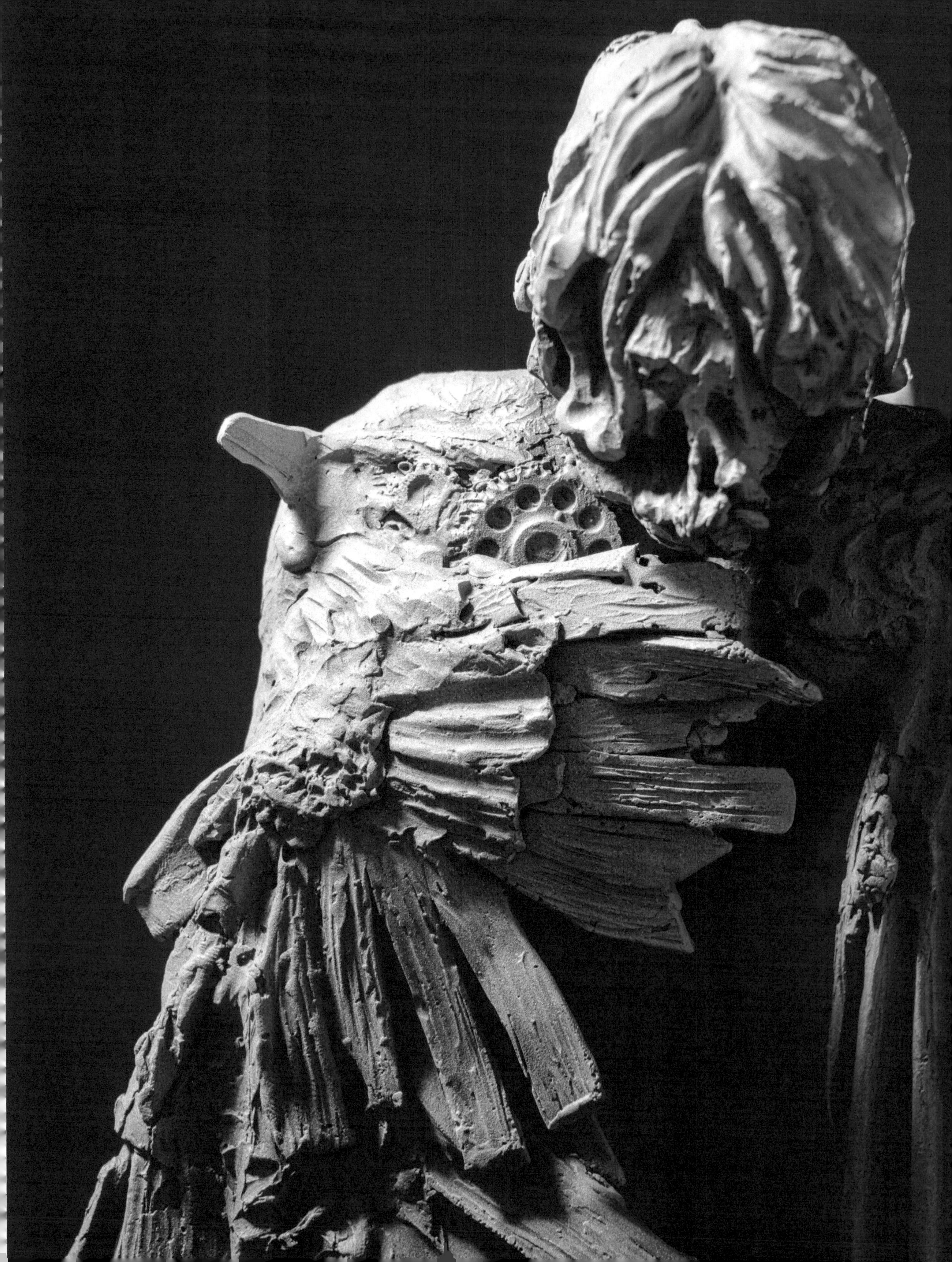

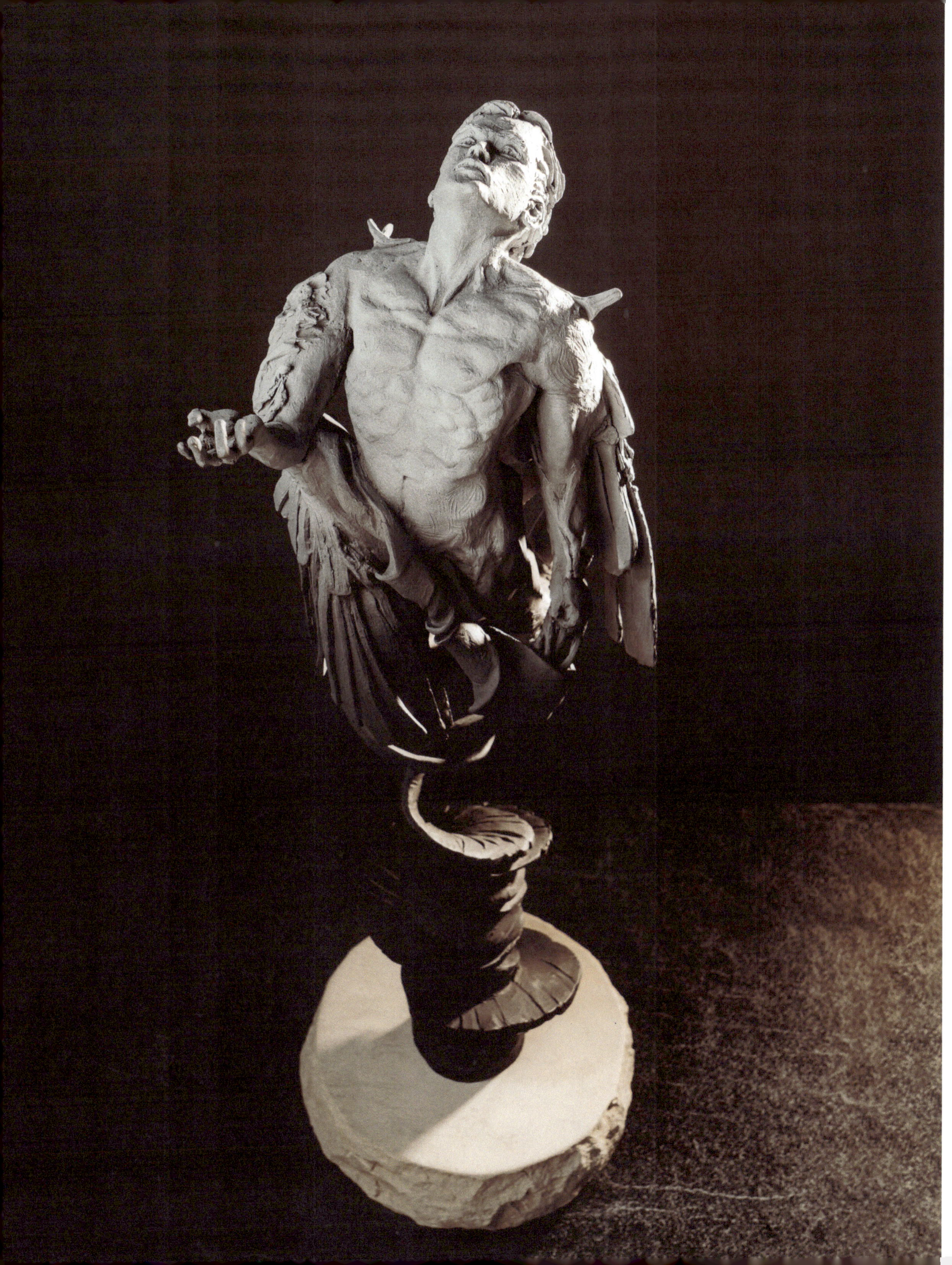

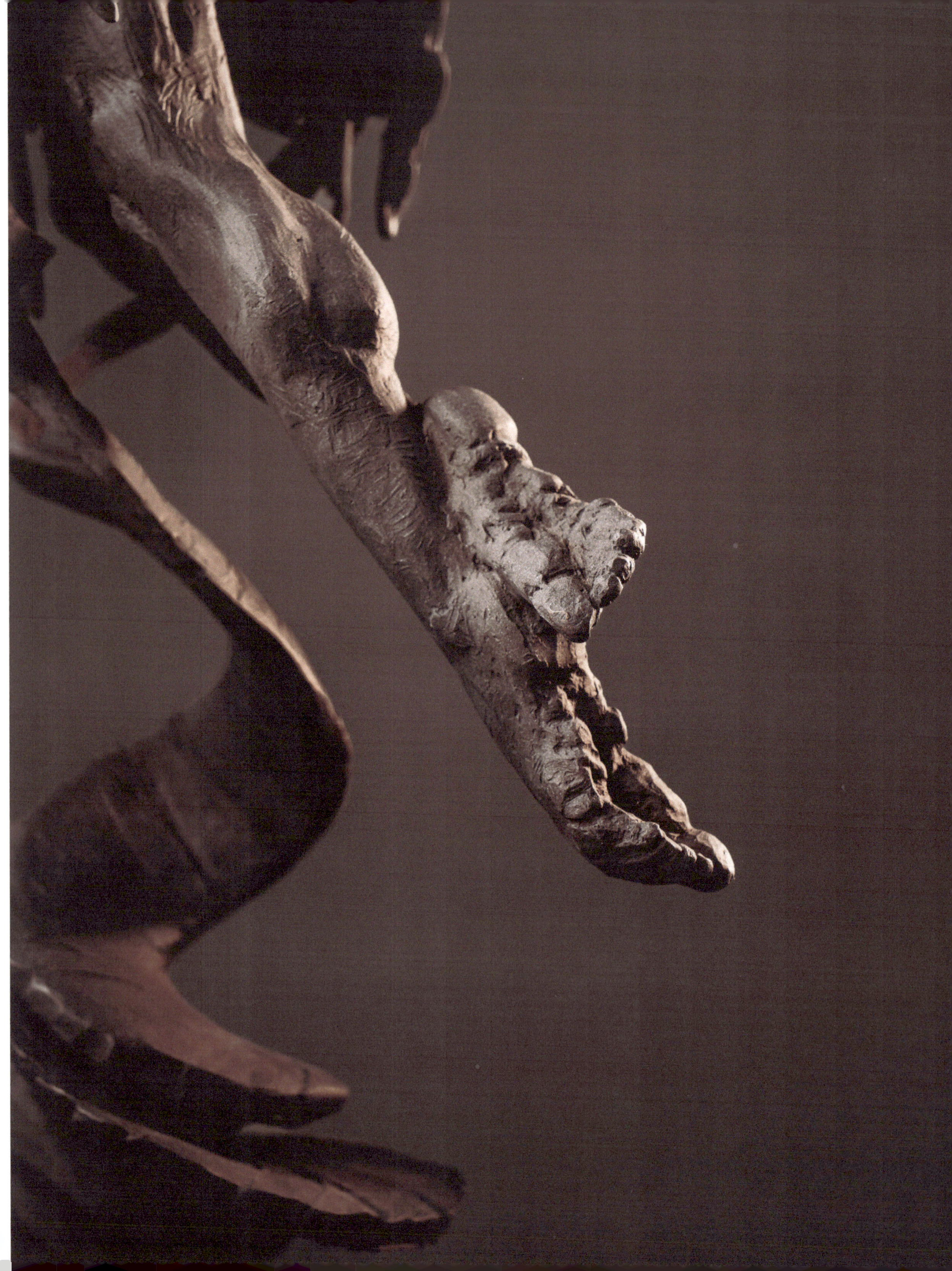

# Sunrise

The story behind Sunrise evolved circumstantially. Three days into a five-day sculpting course, the model failed to show for class. We learned that the woman's sixteen-year-old son had died the previous night in a car accident. This tragic news was devastating.

For some reason, I felt a connection to this woman, and with her son's passing, my excitement for the class, to learn and to sculpt, diminished. Instead, sadness and the jarring question of why overshadowed the studio classroom. The last thing I wanted to do was sculpt. Even gazing at her form was too much.

Death, especially of someone so young, hasn't touched my adult life. I wanted to understand what this woman was experiencing. As the days and weeks passed, I wanted to finish the piece this woman modeled for. But how could I continue? This grieving woman, without her son, was now someone different from that person who modeled for the class. How could I replace that form of the woman with the woman who'd endured such sadness and had to continue her life? How could I honor her loss?

One day in my studio, considering this dilemma, I observed a beam of sunlight falling onto the unfinished sculpture, chasing the shadows away until it seemed the sculpture glowed. As I pondered this beam of light, I discovered the answer. Hope. Hope that emanates into the dark spaces, hope that heals with the promise of brighter days ahead.

The pain of a fresh wound eventually subsides, even if a scar remains. We live in a world dependent on the sun. We crave its light and warmth, which disperses the darkness. Inevitably in this life, we experience loss, yet the memories of those we love strengthen us to lift others. Gaze into the face of Sunrise. Set in the sun, that face will glow. Her face, lifting to the heavens, hands rising, connect to her lost child, a simple gesture focused not on death but on life, on those sacred memories with that precious child.

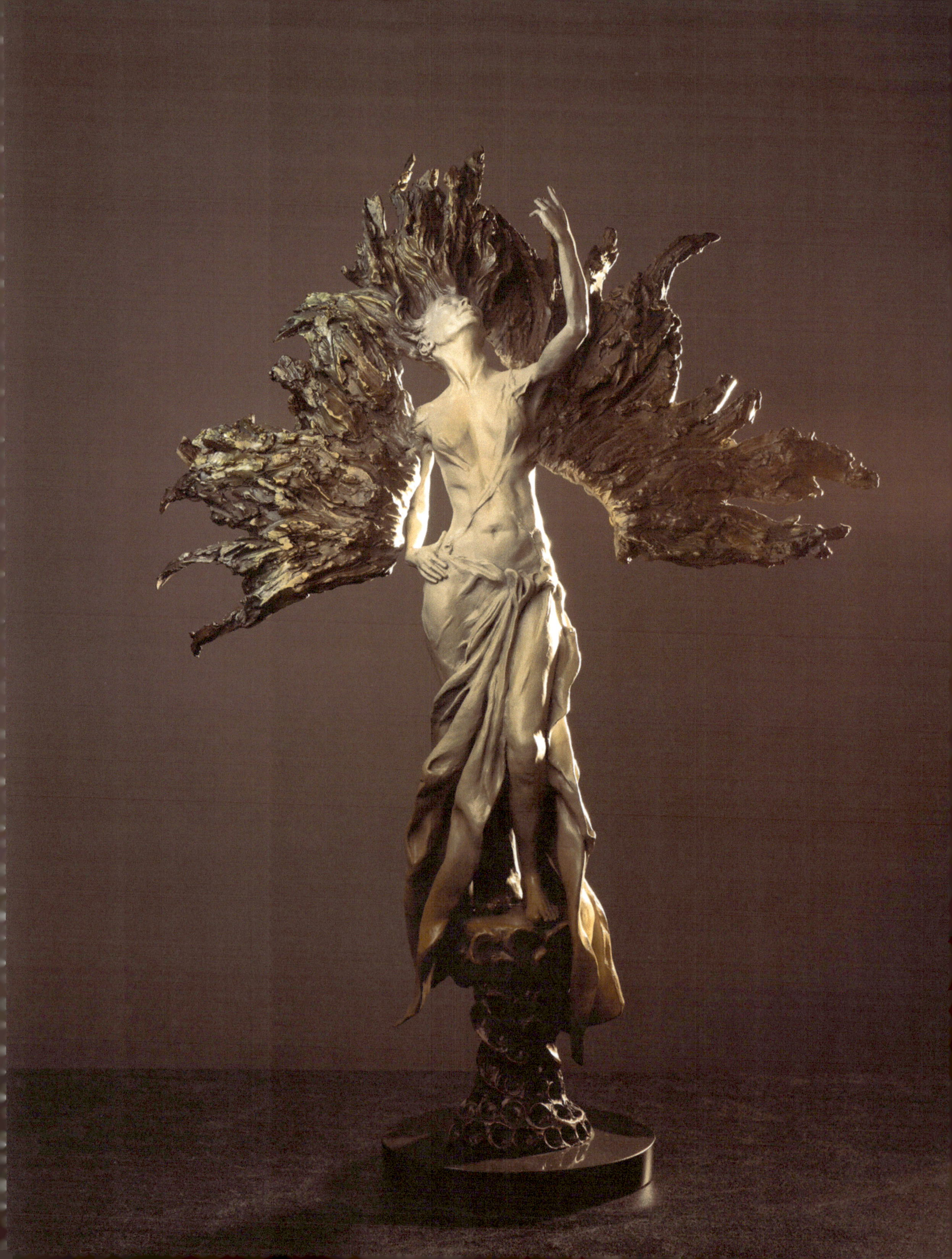

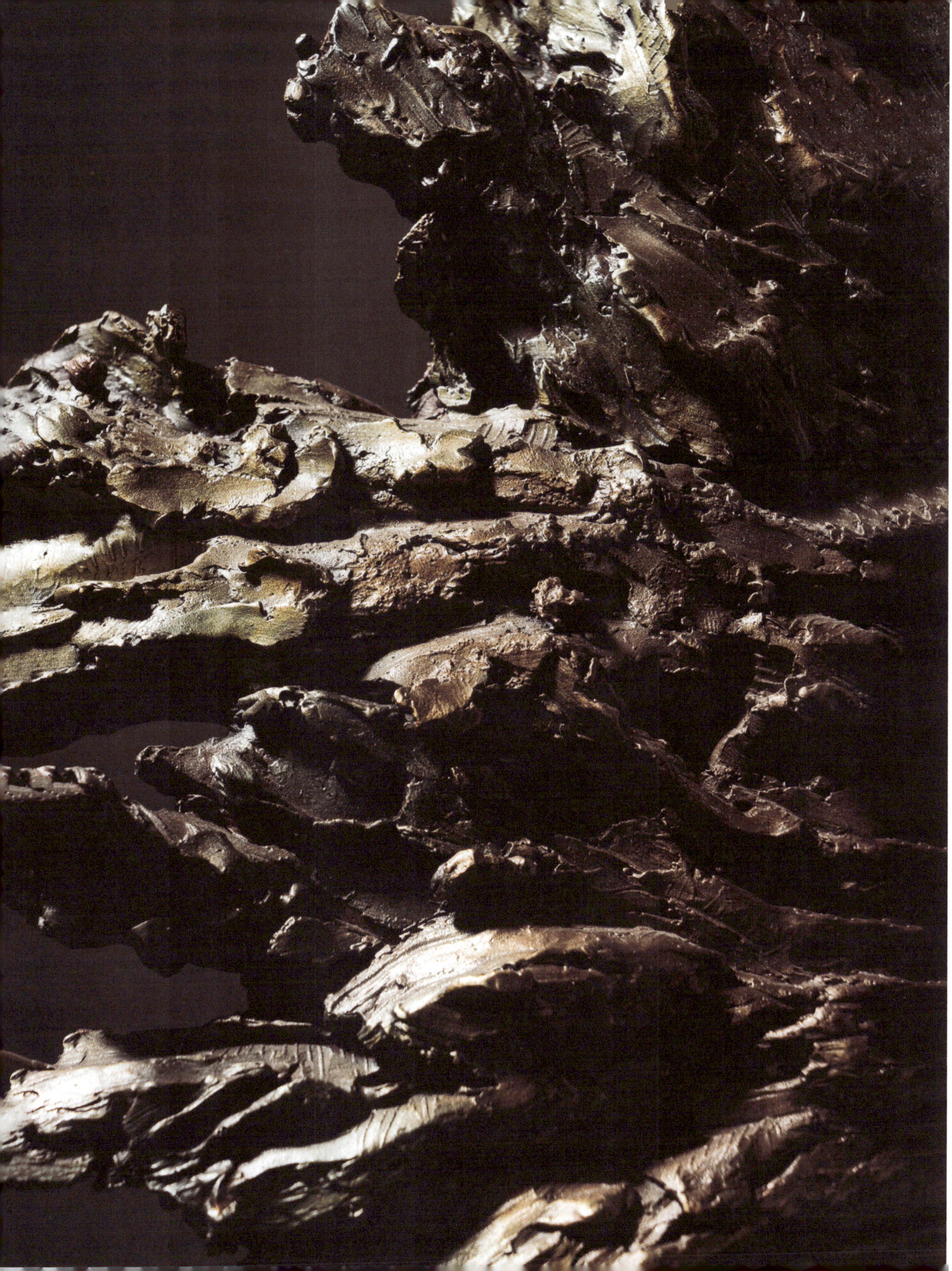

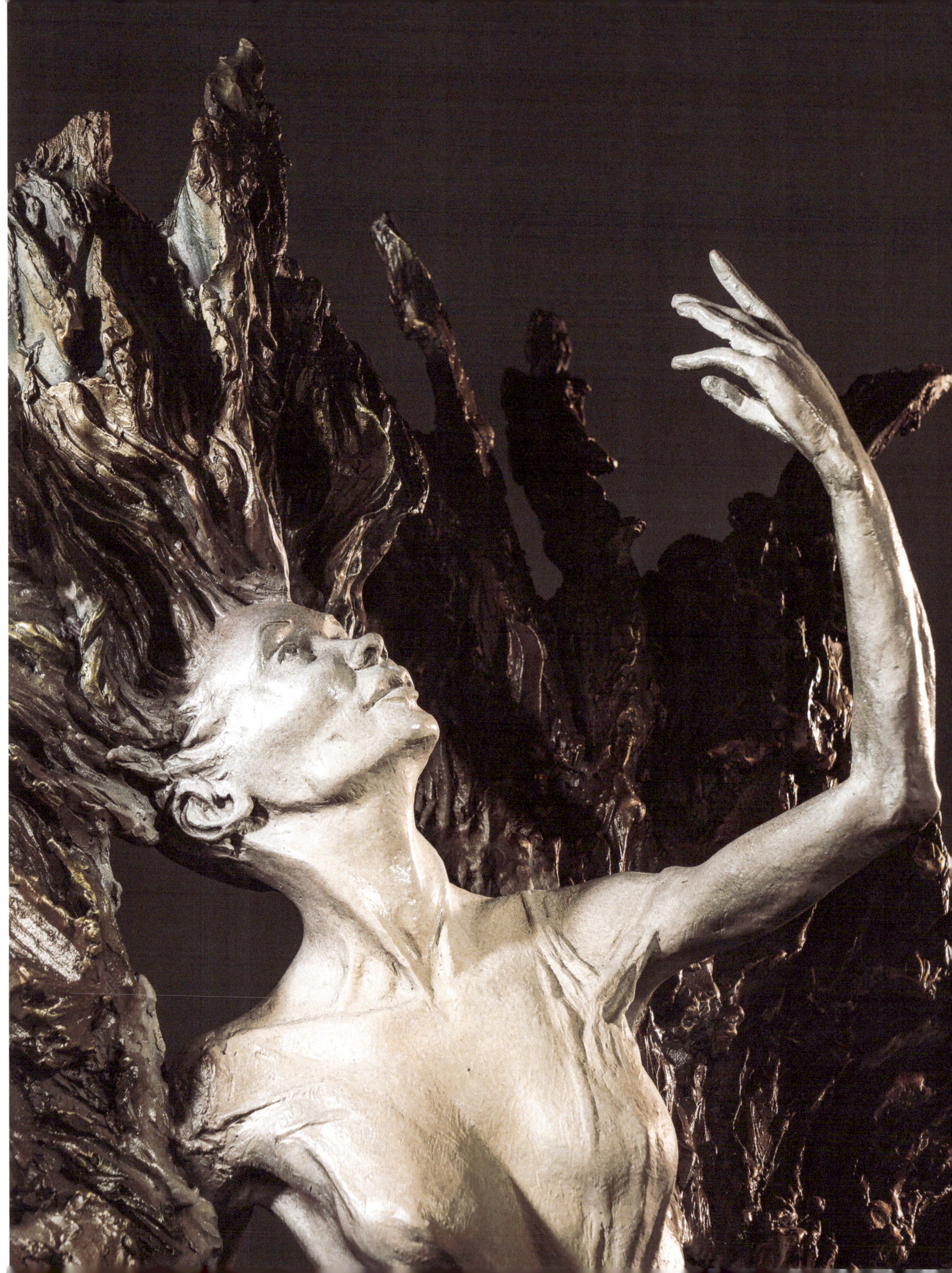

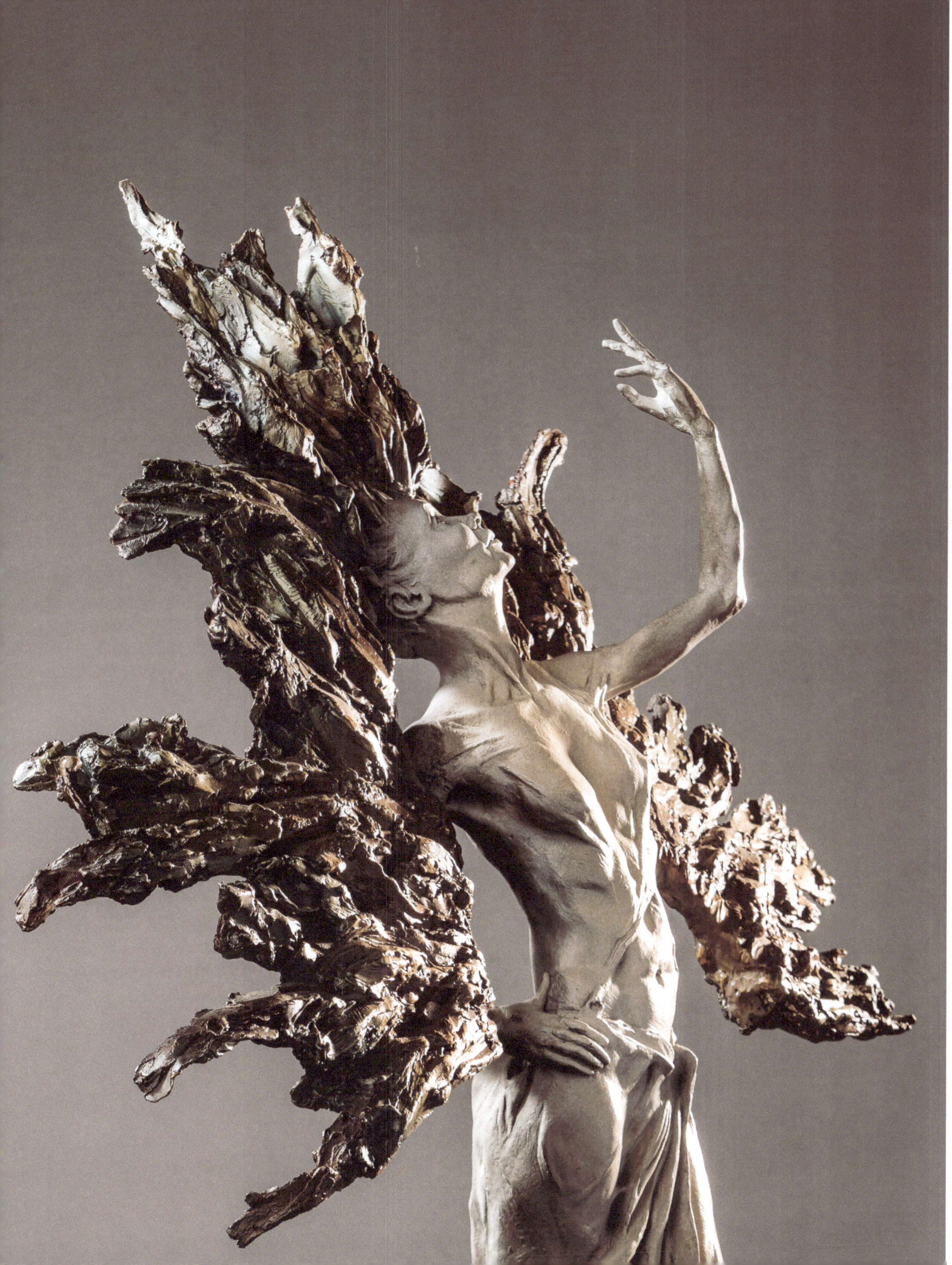

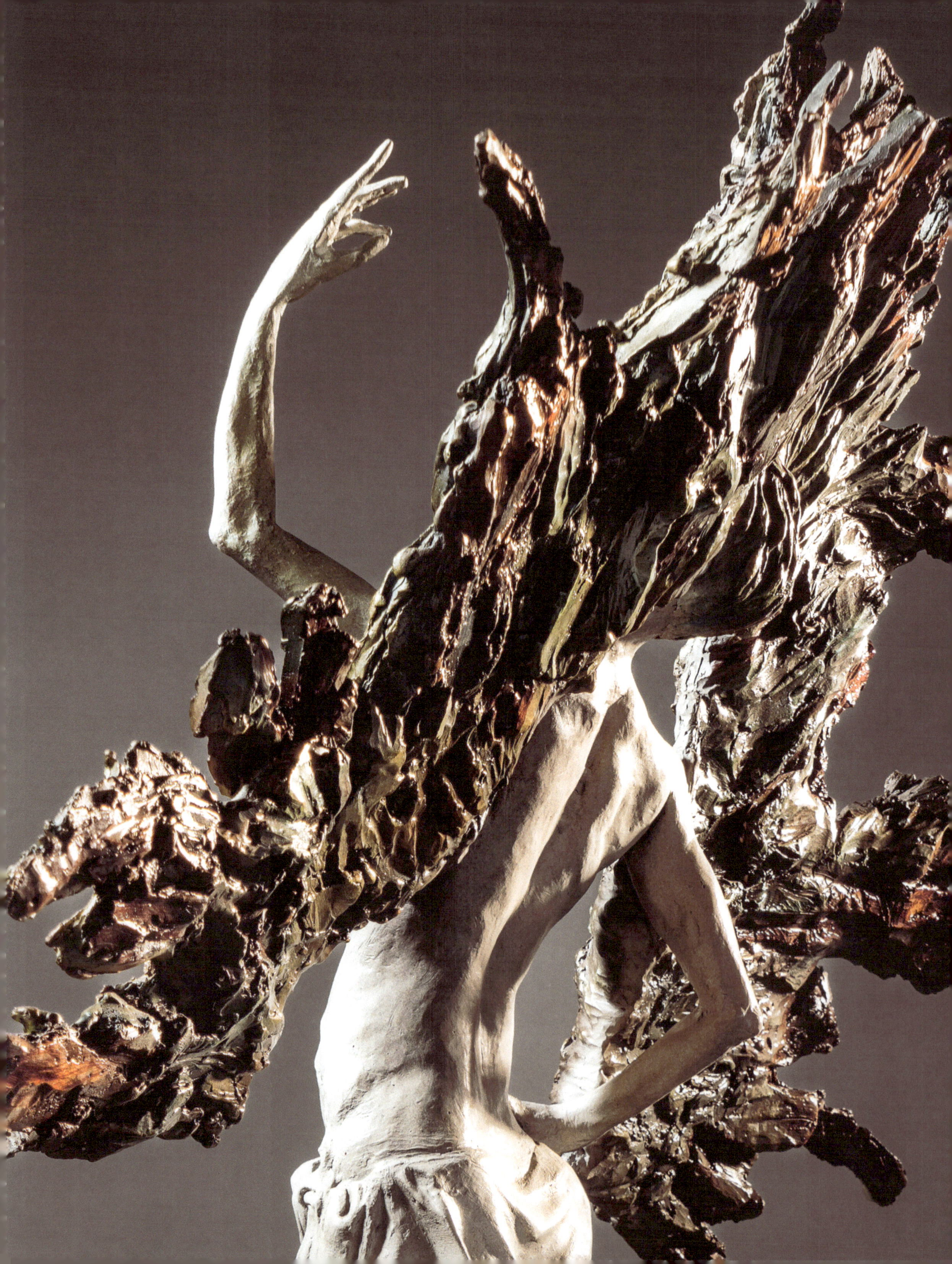

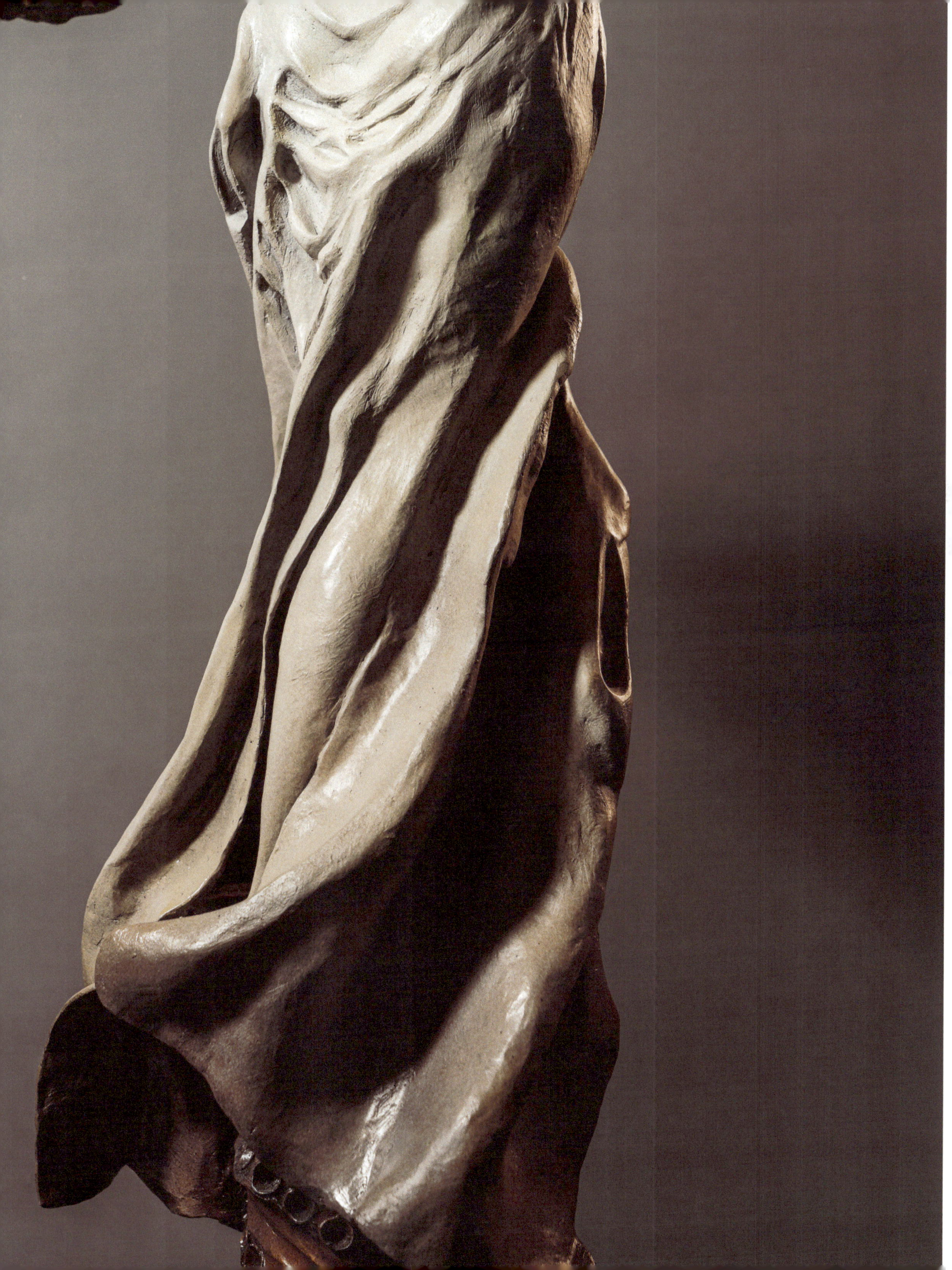

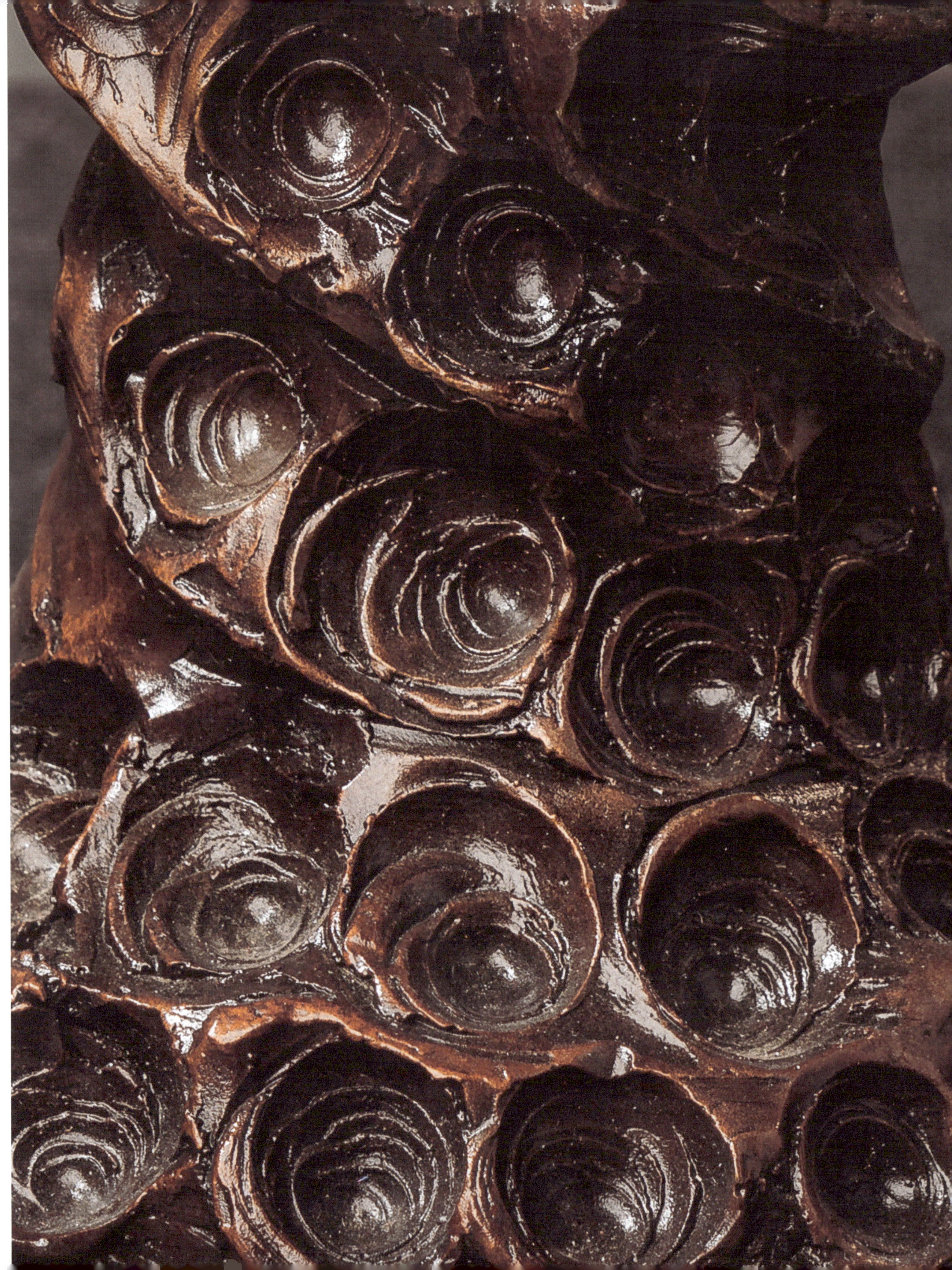

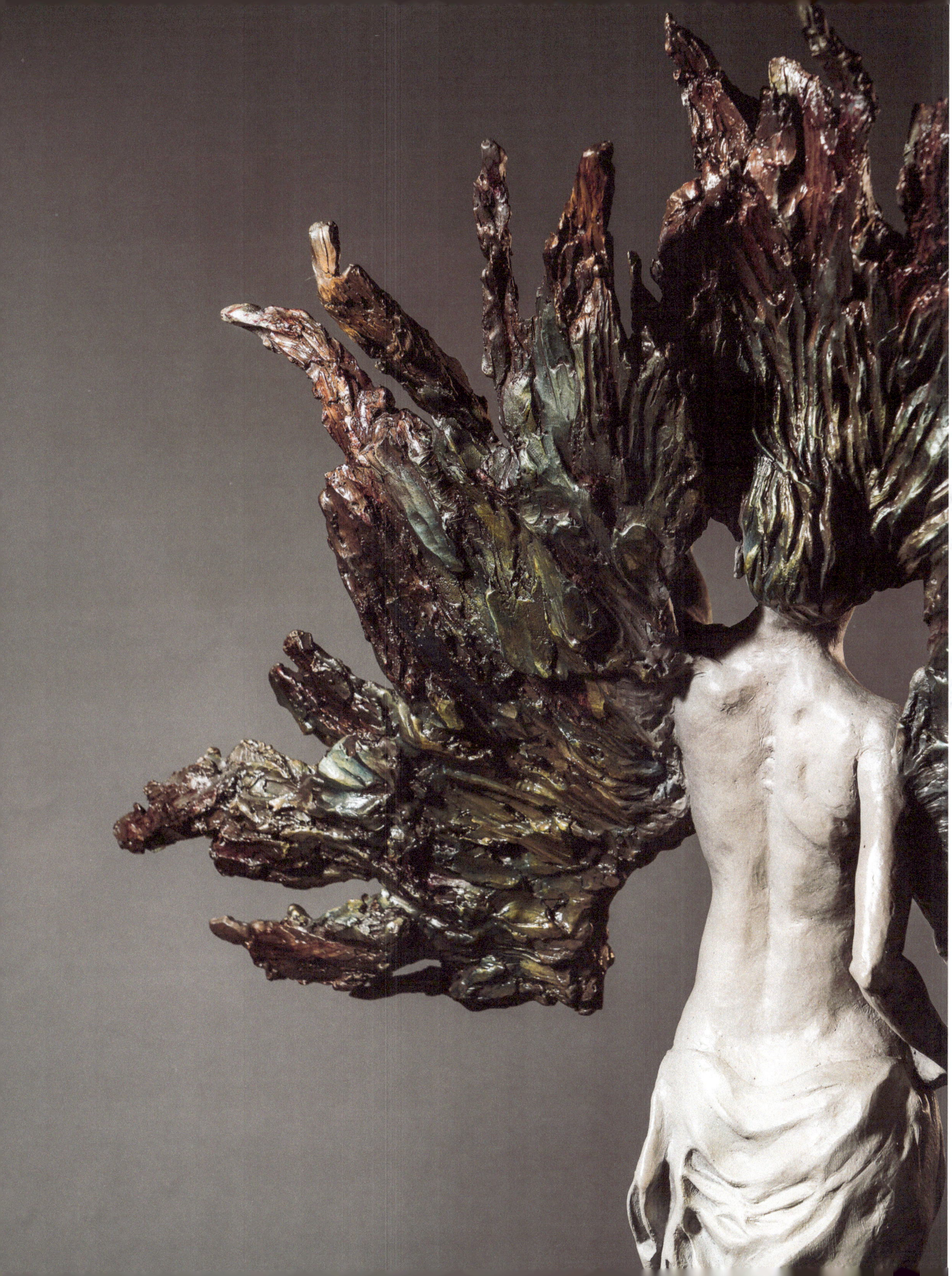

# The Phoenix

The Legend of the Phoenix is associated with Greek mythology, with analogs in Egyptian, Persian, and Judaic cultures. In the legend, the magical, immortal phoenix has the power to regenerate cyclically, doing so by bursting into flames and then rising again from its own ashes.

The phoenix reminds me that I'm a work in progress and that change is not only good but essential. No one is immune from fracturing critical voices and crippling self-doubt. But I've learned not to shrink from adversity. Rather, I stand my ground and rise like the phoenix, more determined than ever.

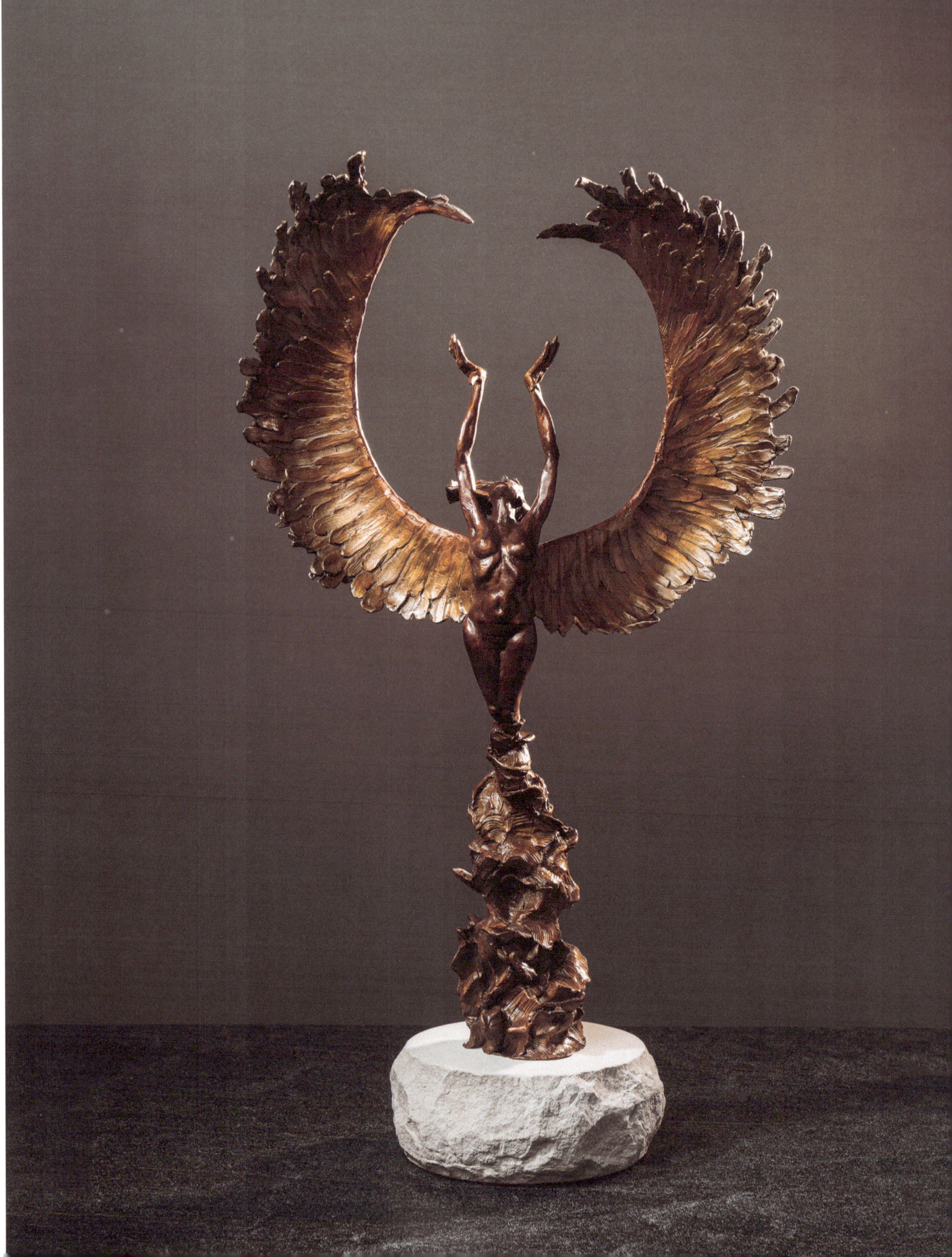

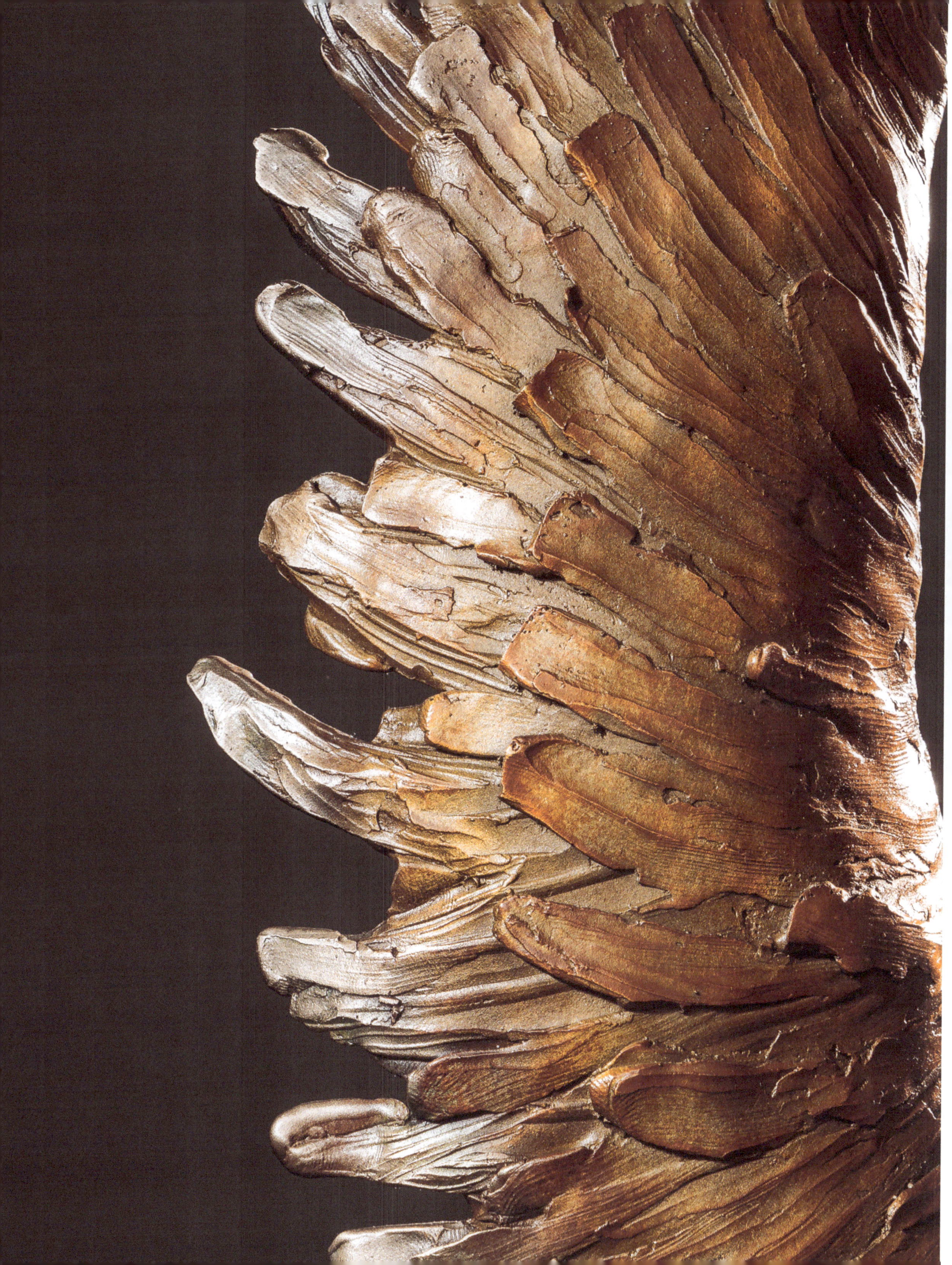

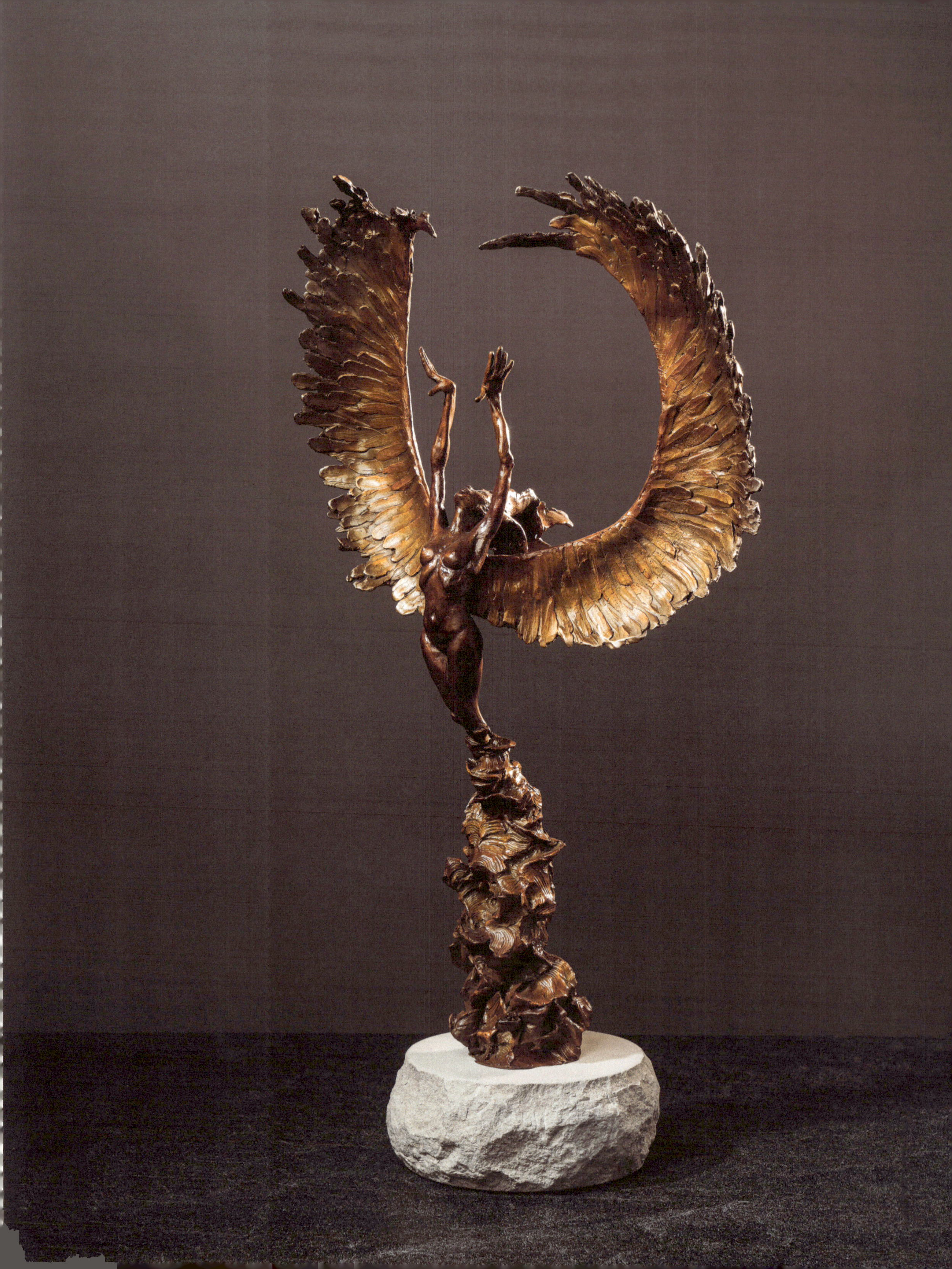

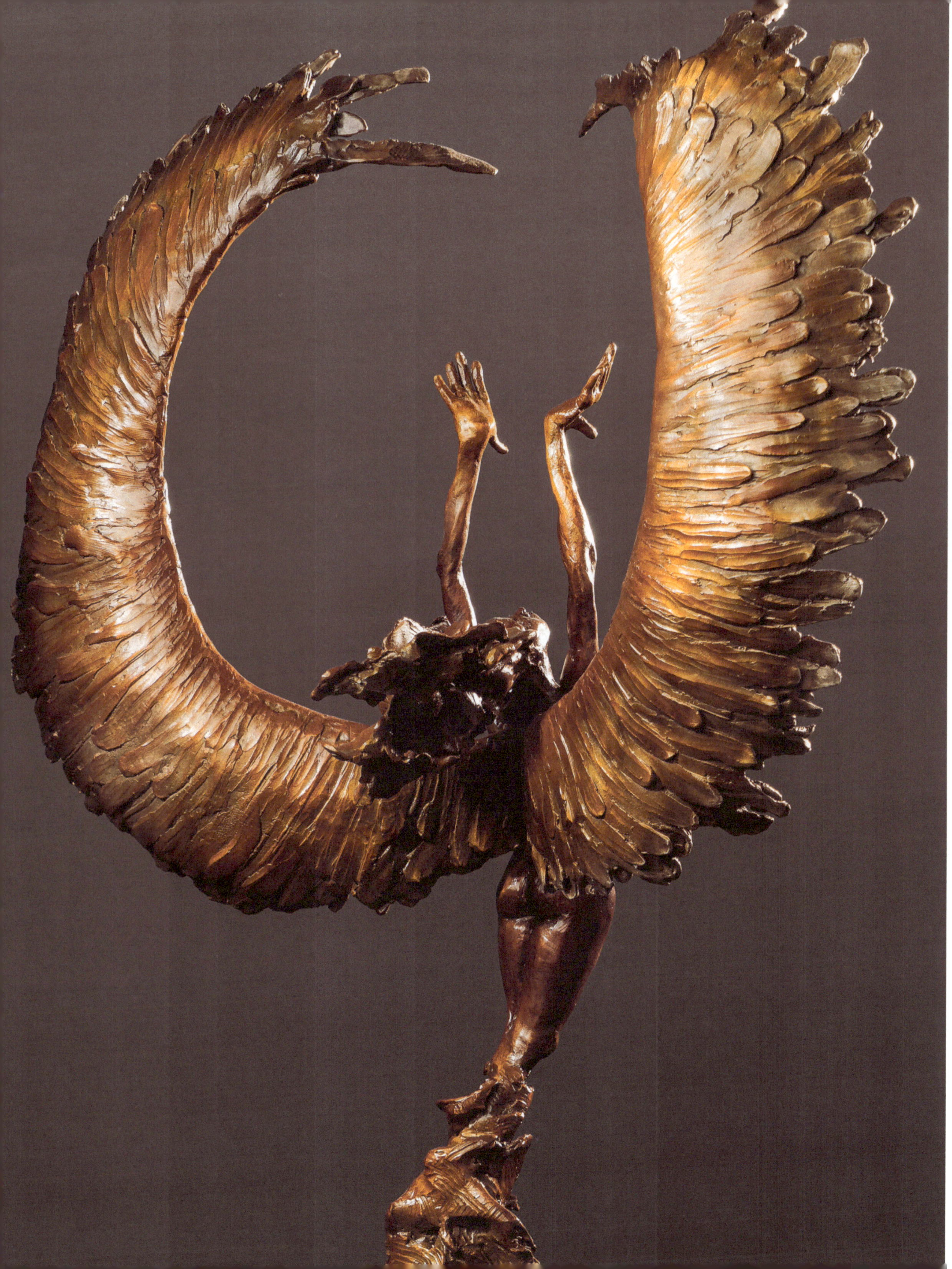

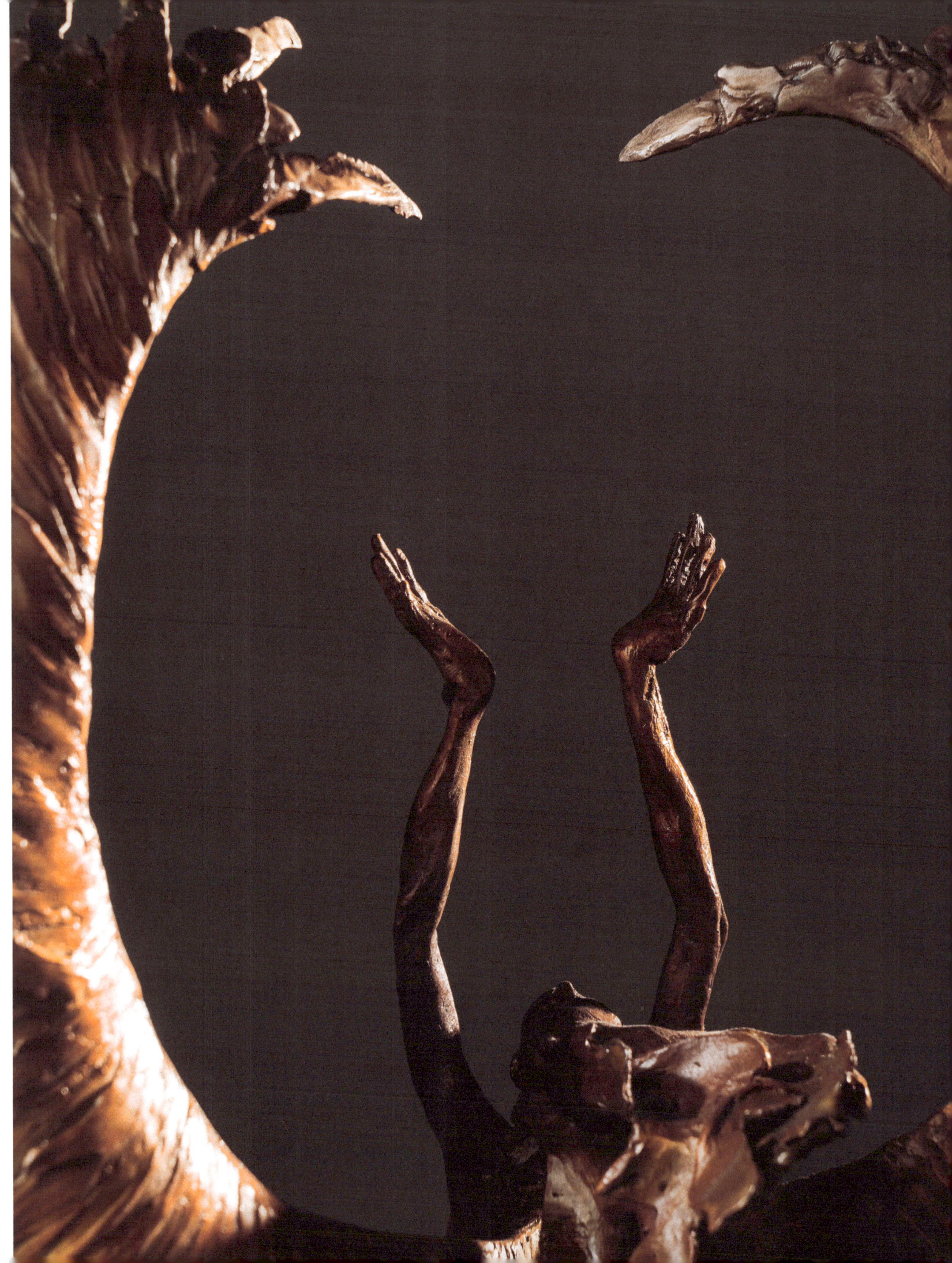

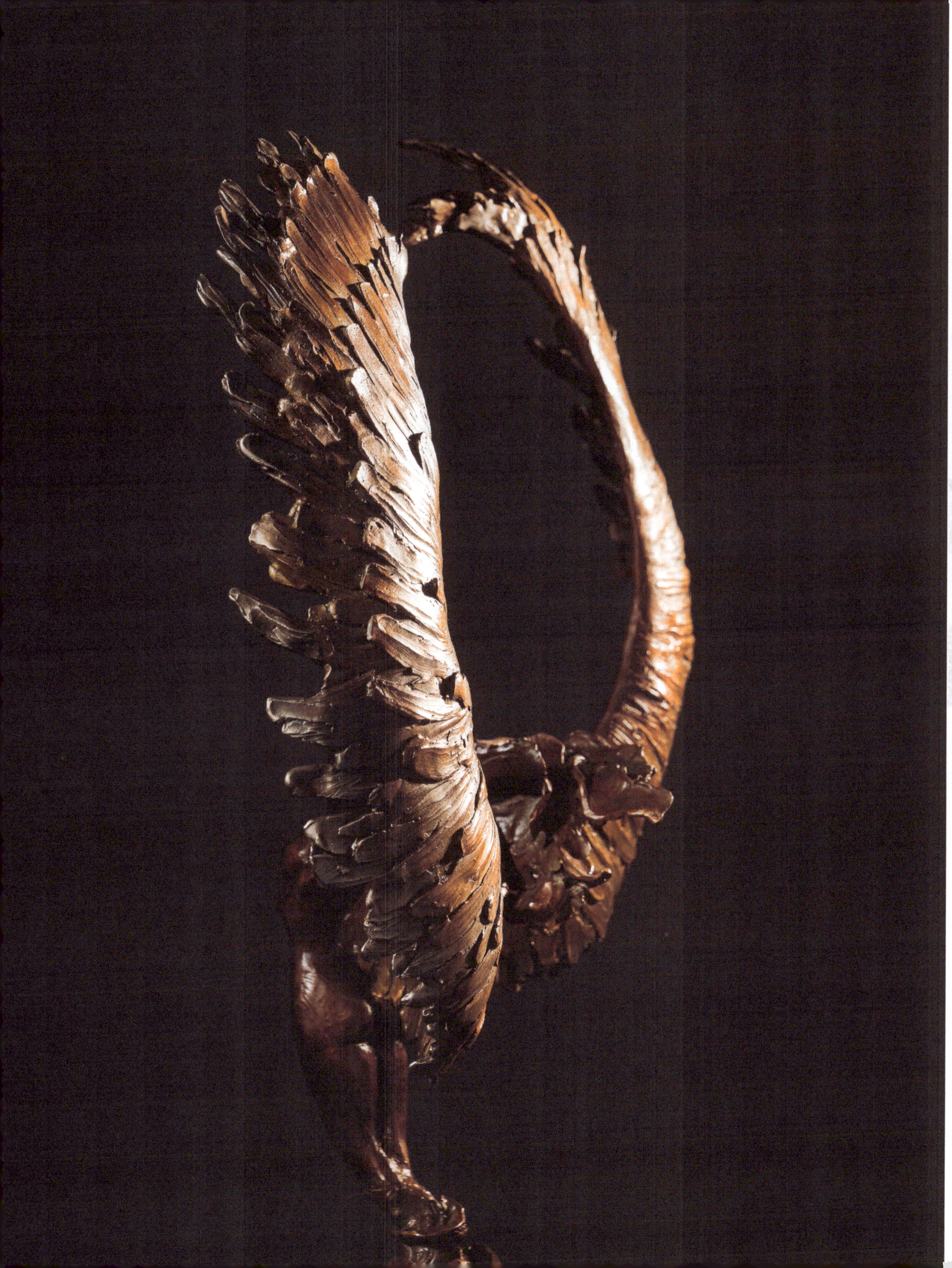

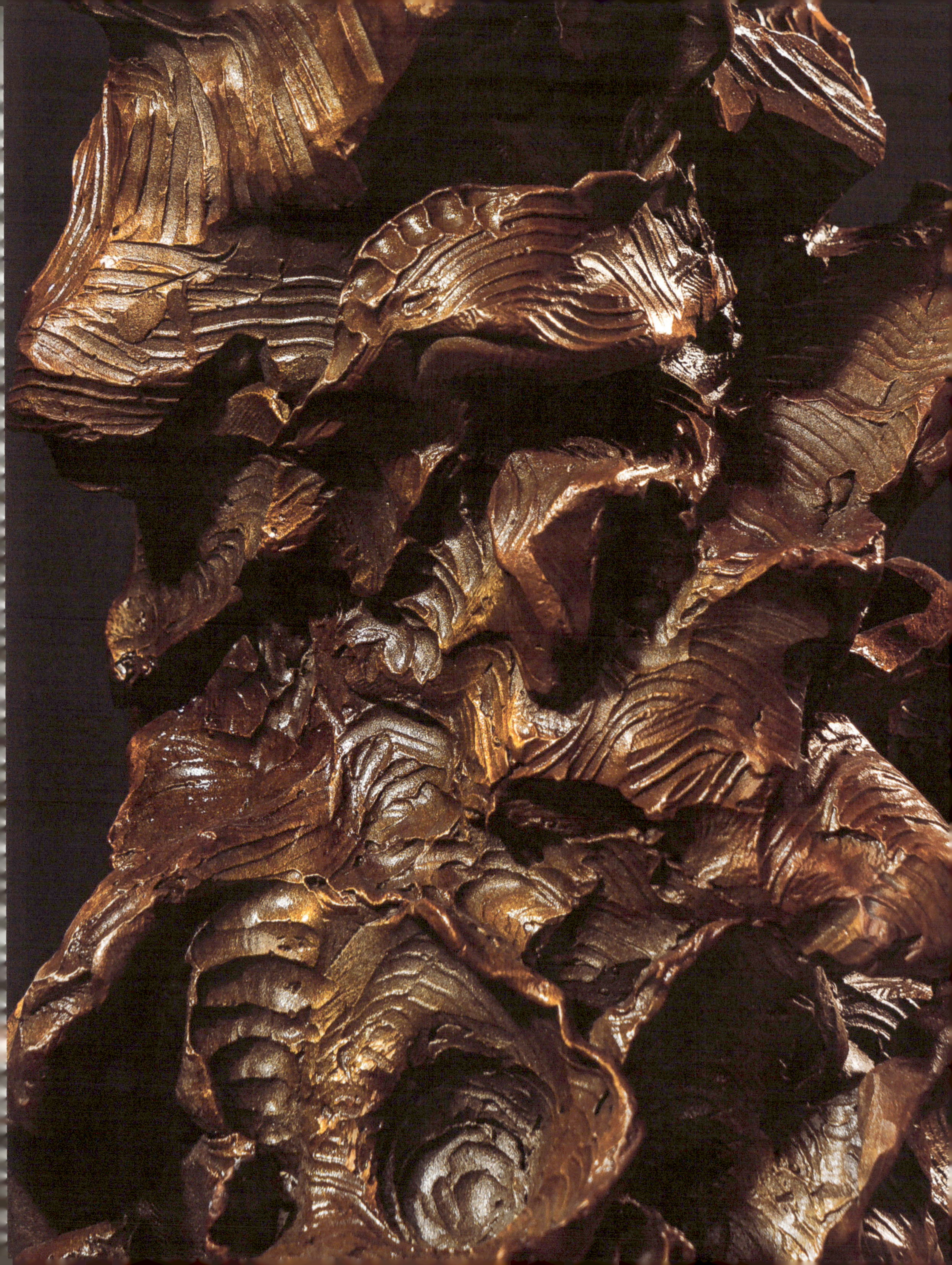

# Leviathan

The idea for Leviathan came from a friend who wanted me to sculpt a dragon. My reaction? I laughed and immediately declined, telling him that there were certain cliched subjects I wanted to avoid sculpting, dragons, and bears being two of them.

A respected sculptor once told me, "Jon, you won't be a legitimate sculptor until you've sculpted a bear." If every sculptor creates a bear, I concluded, then bears are cliché, and dragons can't be that far behind bears. As an artist, I don't want to retread what's been done again and again.

But I could see that this explanation disappointed my dragon-loving friend. I asked him why he wanted a dragon. I didn't anticipate his response. He wanted a dragon, specifically a fire dragon because it was his Chinese zodiac. He told me more about how his wife is Chinese and how marrying into a culture different from his own was initially a struggle. However, over time he began to appreciate and embrace Chinese culture, discovering more about himself and, in turn, experiencing a surprising sense of belonging and wholeness.

The sculpture's name references a sea monster, the most powerful in the ocean, the embodiment of chaos who feasts on the damned after this life. The Book of Job describes the Leviathan as a fierce, untamable beast with impenetrable armor and a mouth full of sharp teeth.

The sculpture depicts a man intertwined with the Leviathan. At first glance, it may appear that they're struggling against each other. Or are they supporting each other?

One theme I frequently return to is deceitful eyes. We interpret the world, often very quickly and inaccurately. One way we do this is through our judgements about race and culture, even when people have no control over the color of their skin or the circumstance in which they're born. But we act as if others have control over these aspects of life. We use what our eyes see to form inaccurate opinions that divide us.

My hope is that this sculpture will unite. As I've gone out into the world and learned more about people seemingly different from me, I realize there is more that unites than divides. We need each other, and like my friend, we need the beauty of different cultures to feel whole. If we rely less on our eyes and more on our minds, we can heal hurtful prejudice and cruel actions. We can unite with the Leviathan. We can become greater than we ever could on our own.

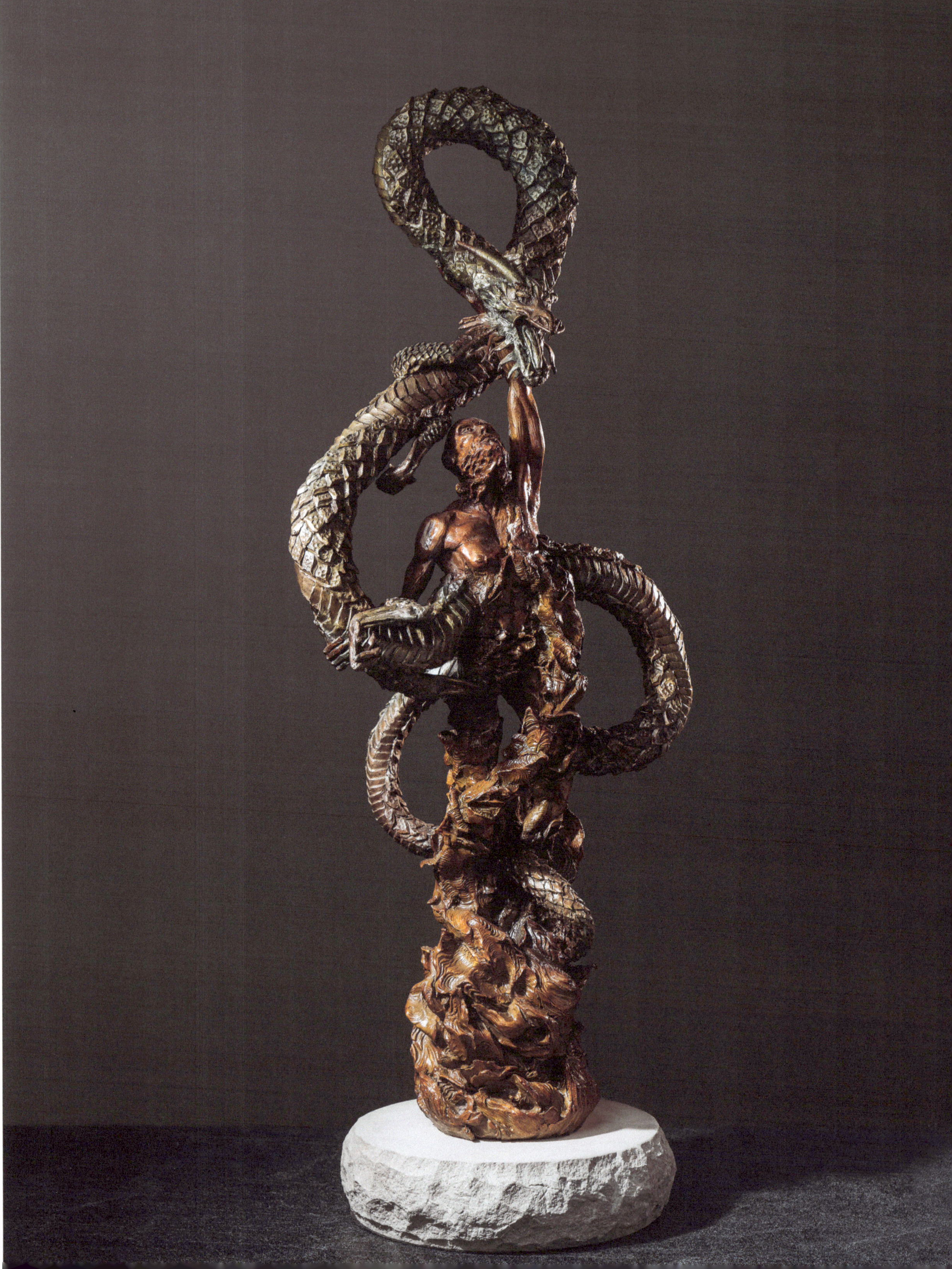

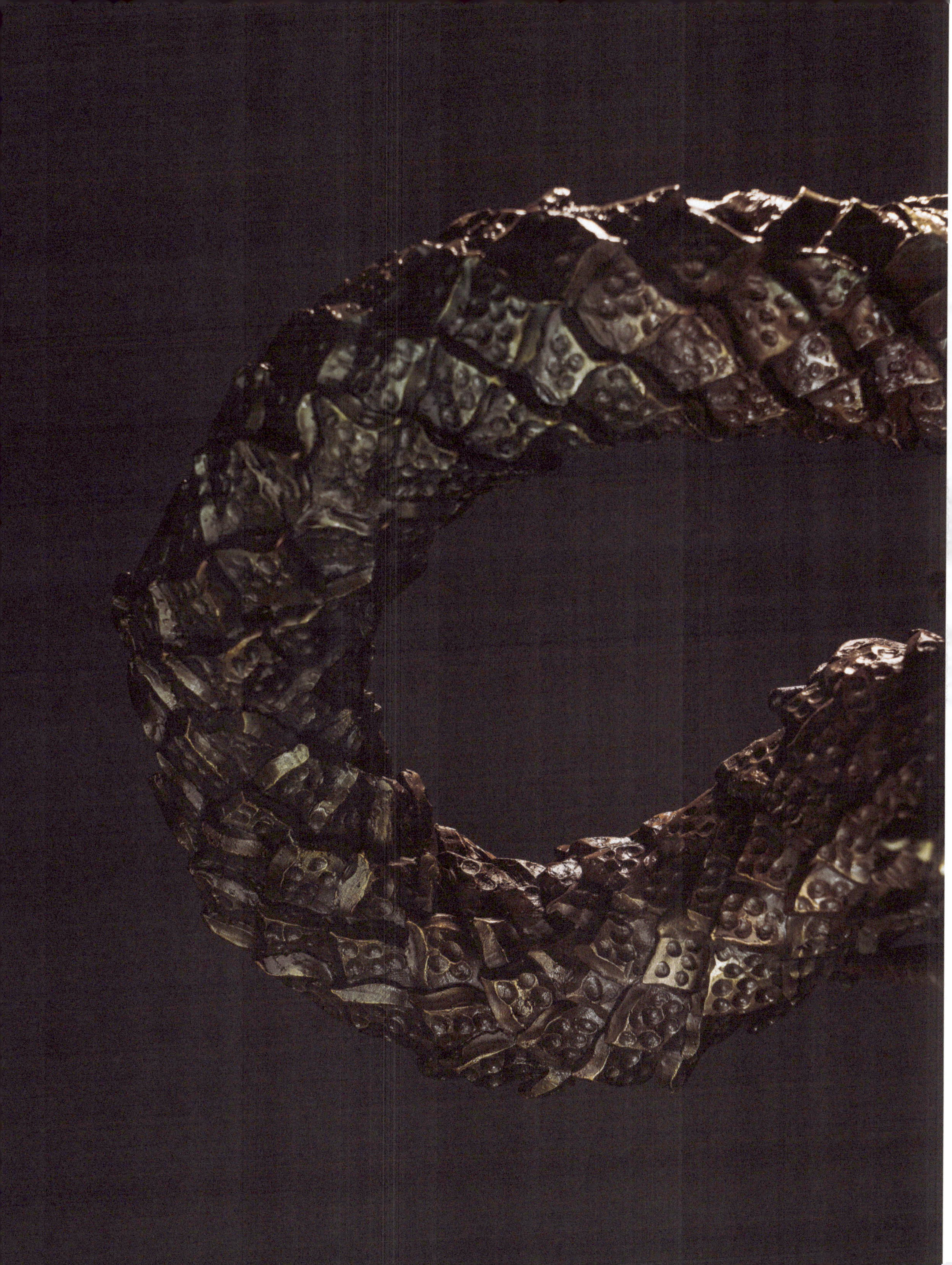

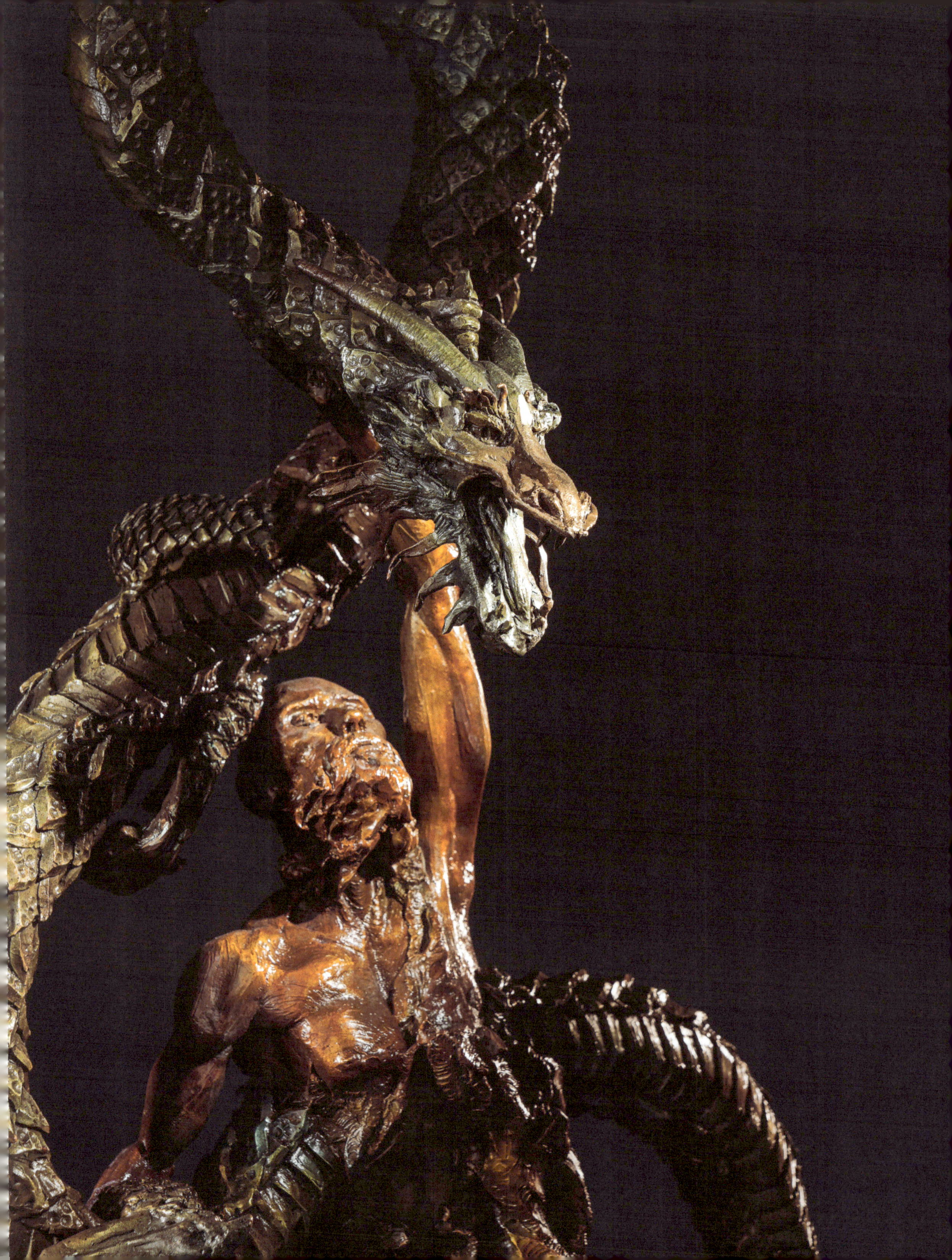

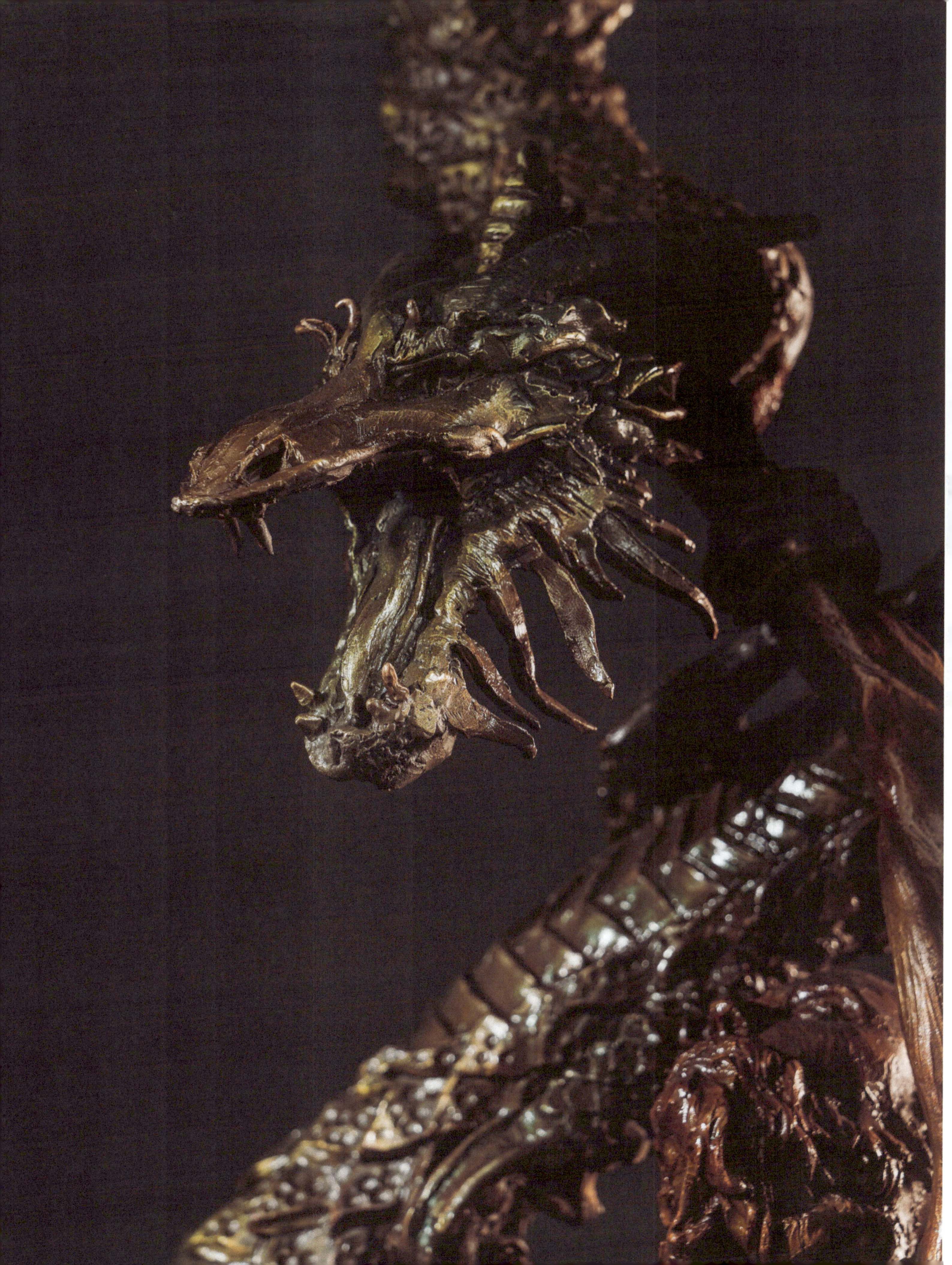

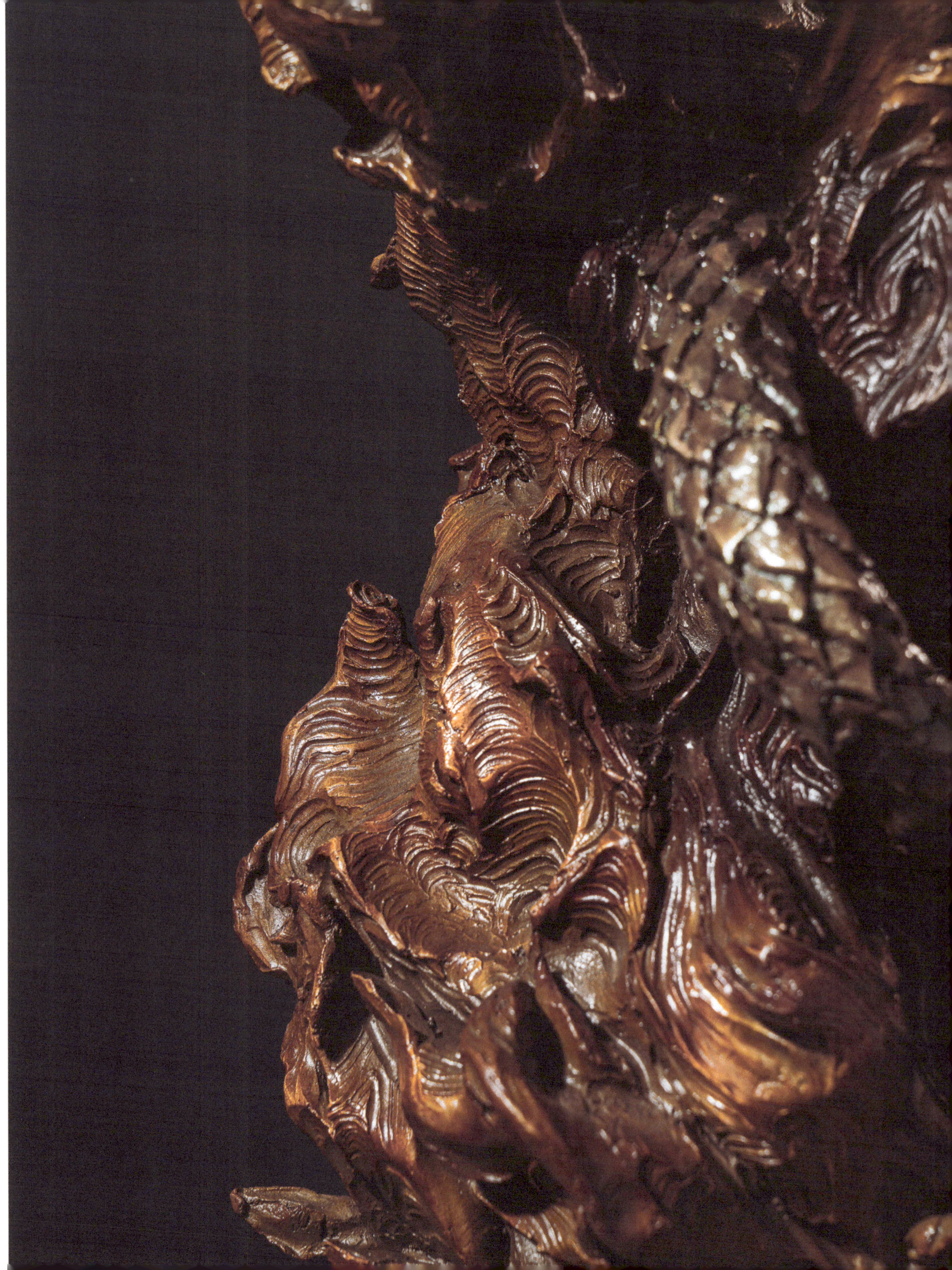

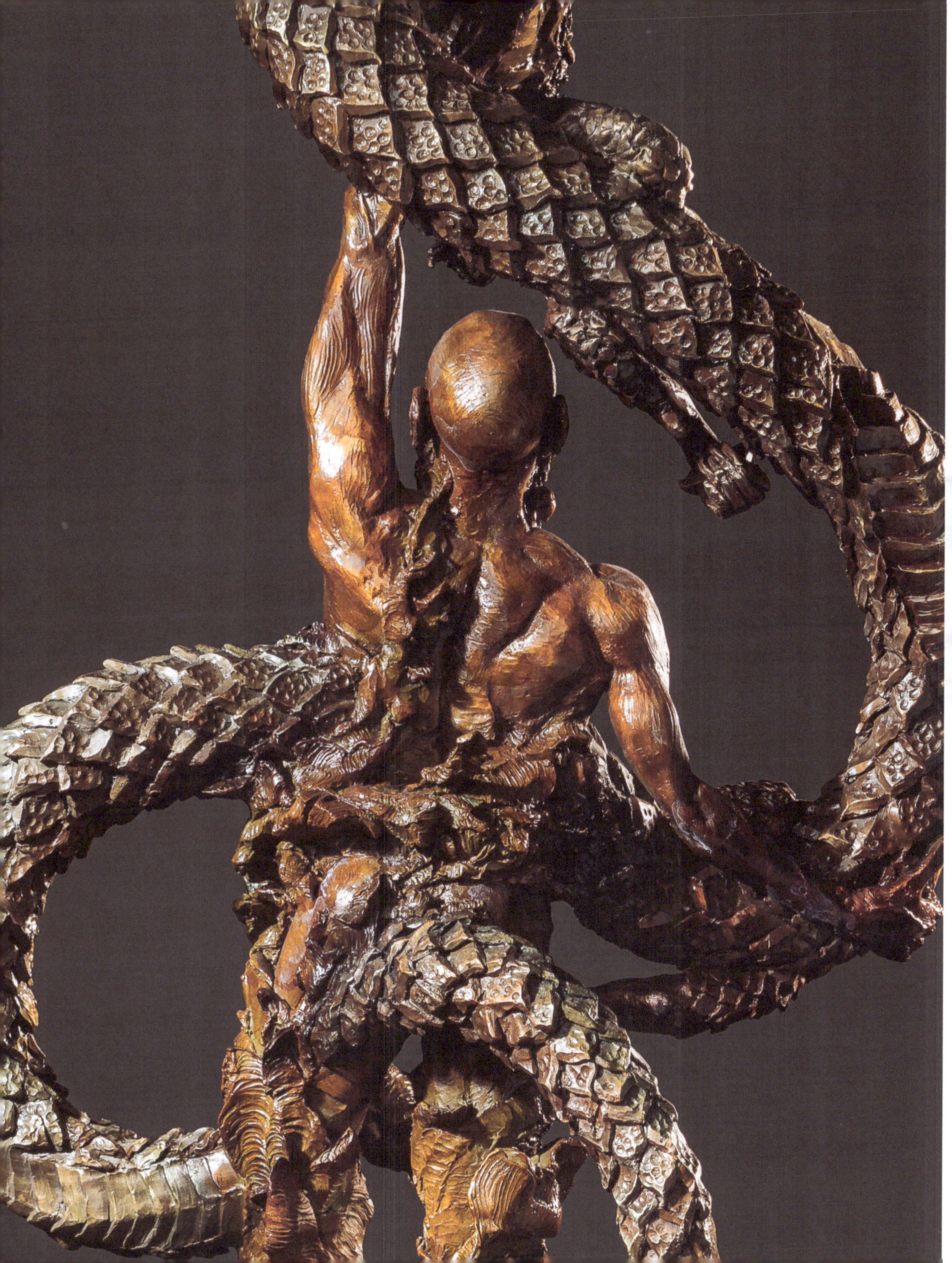

# Sunset

Sunset. For some, it's a somber moment of self-evaluation and judgement: How was the day spent? What opportunities were lost? What was left unfinished?

Sunset is not about that. Instead, this sculpture attempts to capture the beauty of that moment as the sun dips below the horizon: the softening light, the pink blush of clouds, and the reds and oranges painting the majestic sky. And the realization of that moment, the day behind us, like every other day, drifting into the past.

I hope this sculpture exudes satisfaction and acceptance. Not all of life is a careful and predictable plan. Life is erratic, chaotic, and bursting with surprises, and only by embracing life's volatility can we conquer. And when the last trace of purple fades from the heavens, and the moon rises like an incandescent disk, we can say: I am good enough!

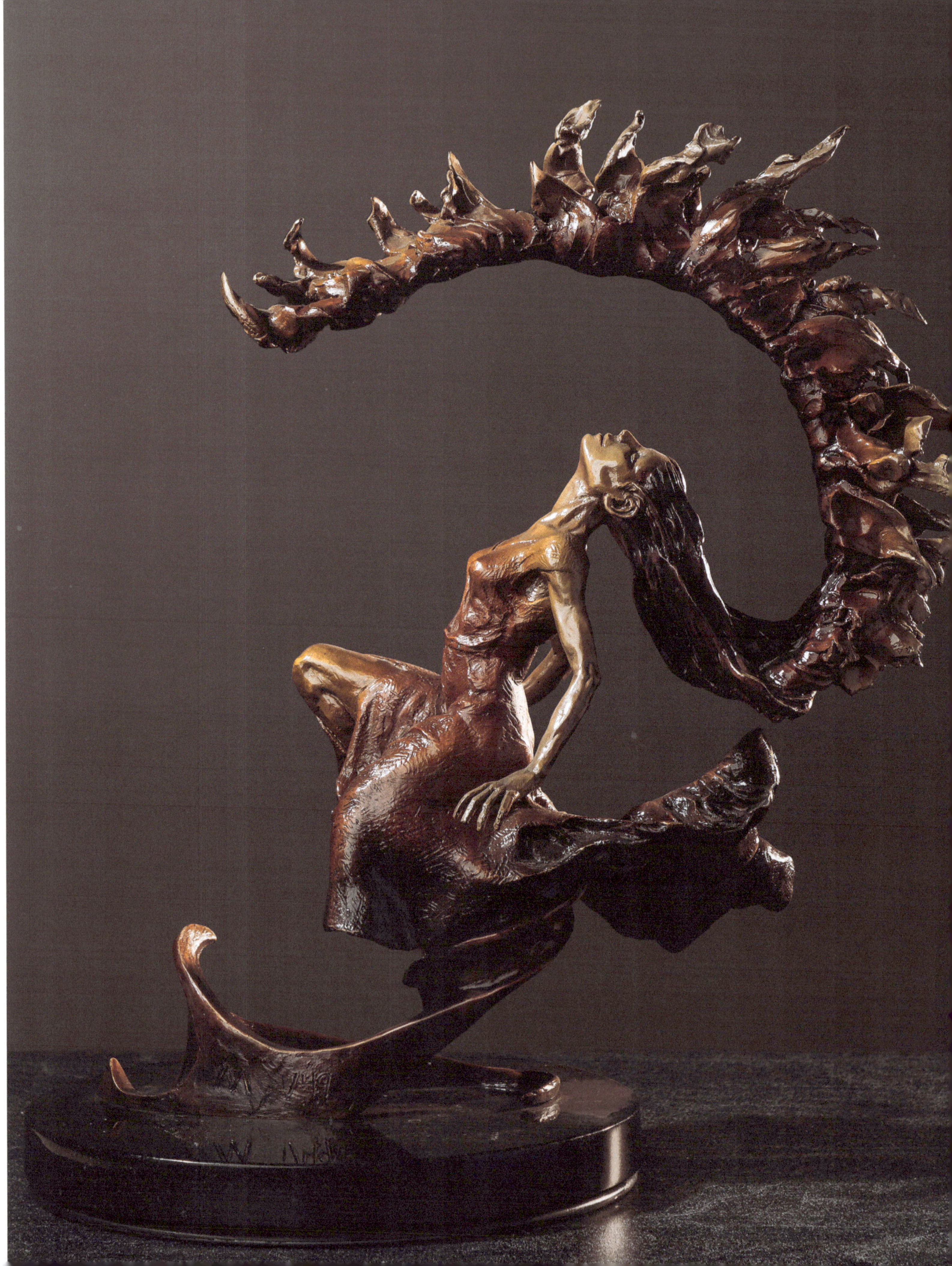

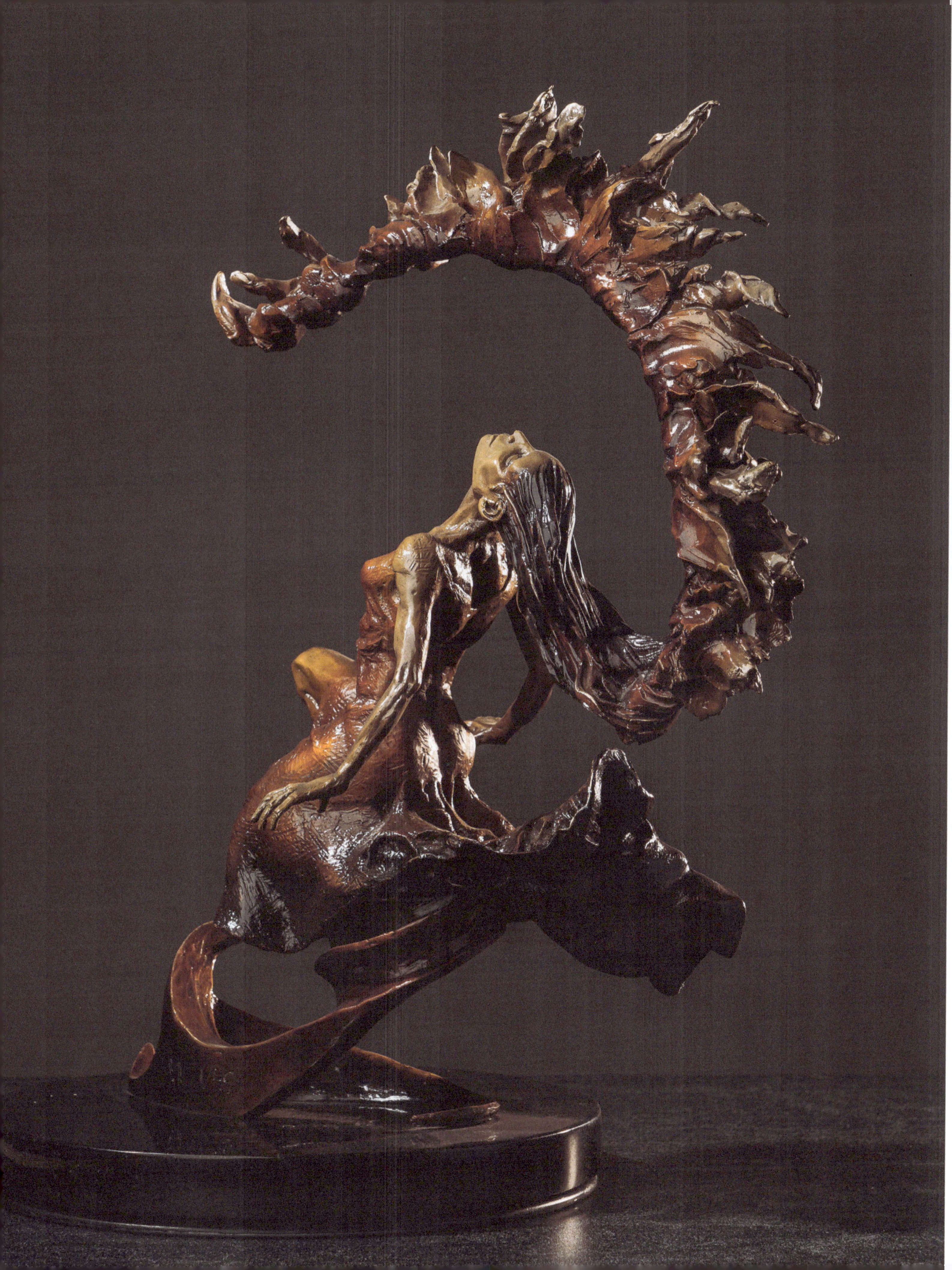

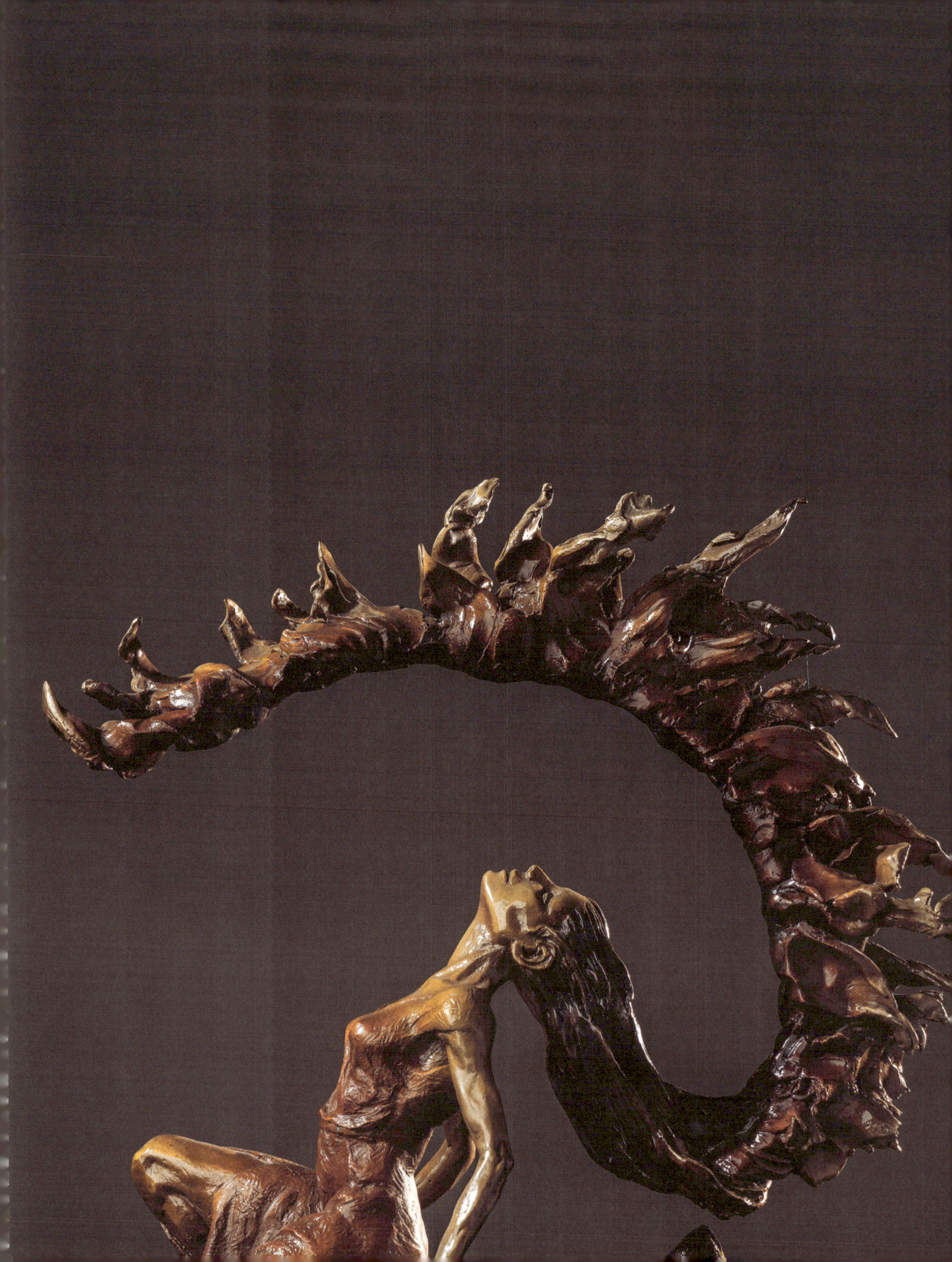

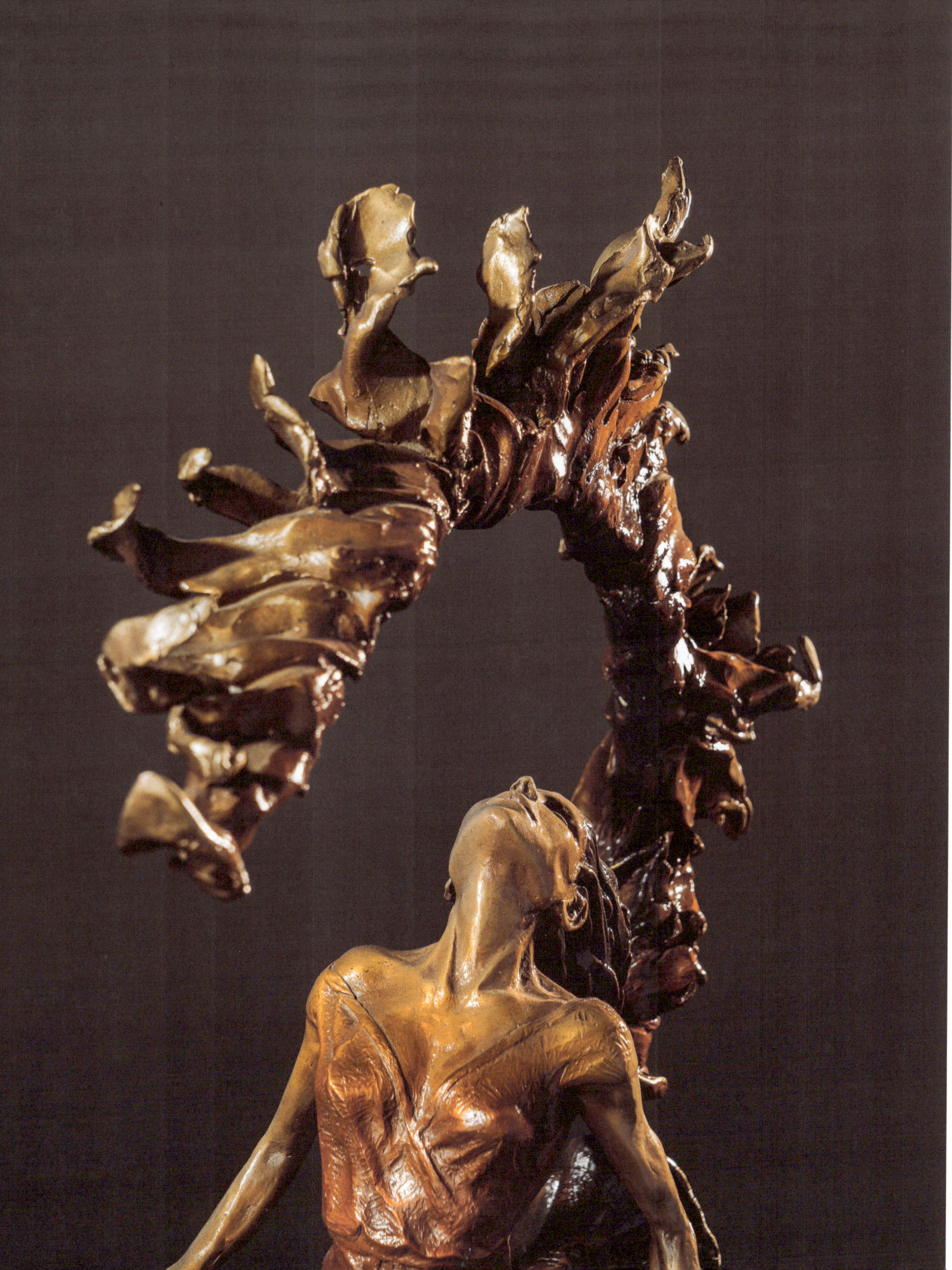

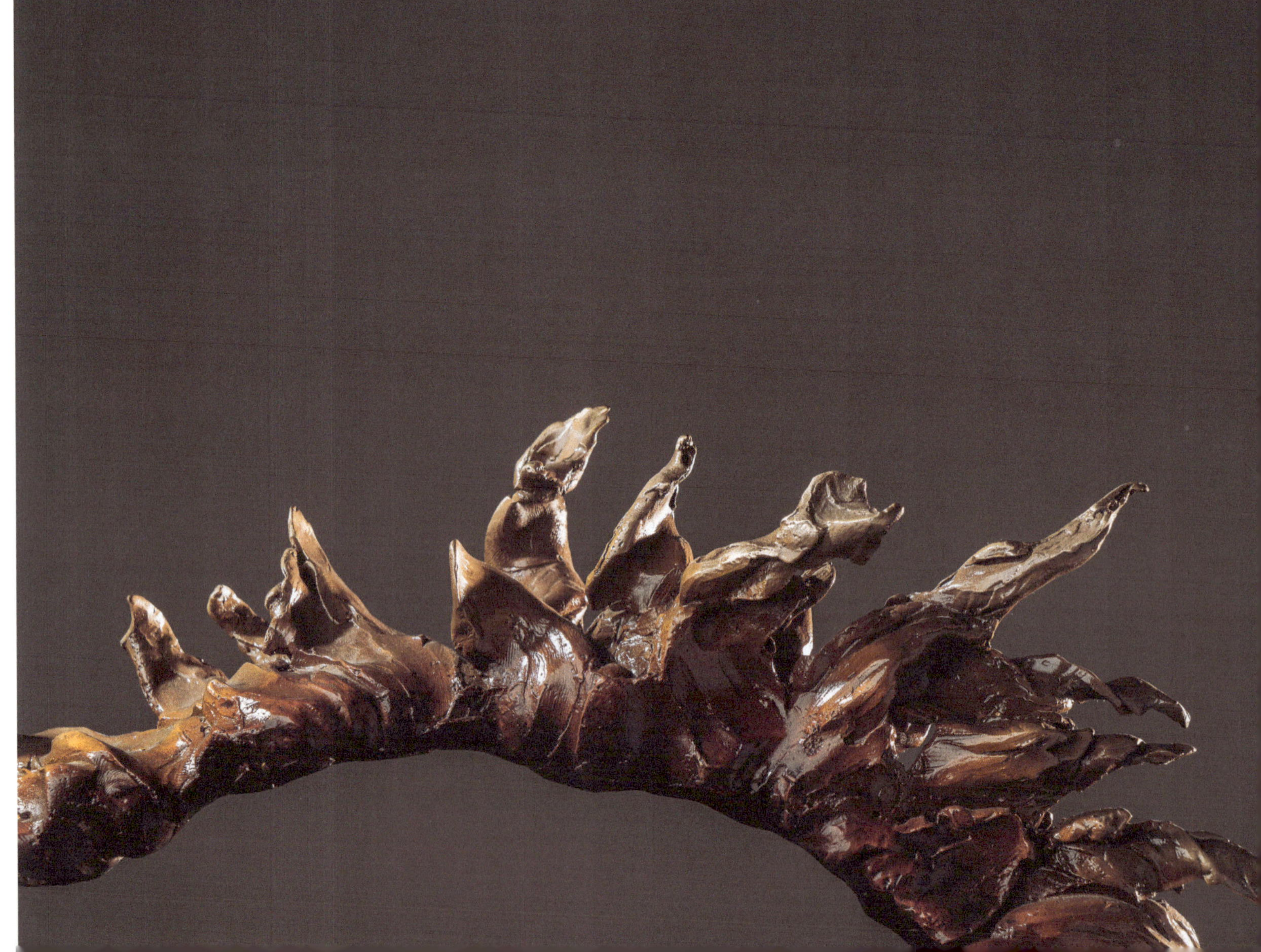

## Storyteller

People often ask where I find ideas for my sculptures. The answer is important. Where do the ideas originate? From people, from conversations, from books, from stories. Ideas, if I feel passionate about them, churn in my mind until I commit to providing them a physical form.

The challenge is transforming those ideas, those thoughts, into physical representations—a kind of puzzle requiring time. Often, with only a budding idea, I begin to sculpt, the energy from my hands transferring to the clay to initiate the creative process. Thoughts, shapes, and ideas form. And even I, as the creator, marvel at the process.

Storyteller returns to the reason I sculpt: to tell stories. I sculpted a hula dancer because dance is one of the earliest forms of storytelling, told through movement and music to pass crucial information from one generation to another.

The story is powerful. It allows each of us to contribute something profound. It unites us through the knowledge that makes us human.

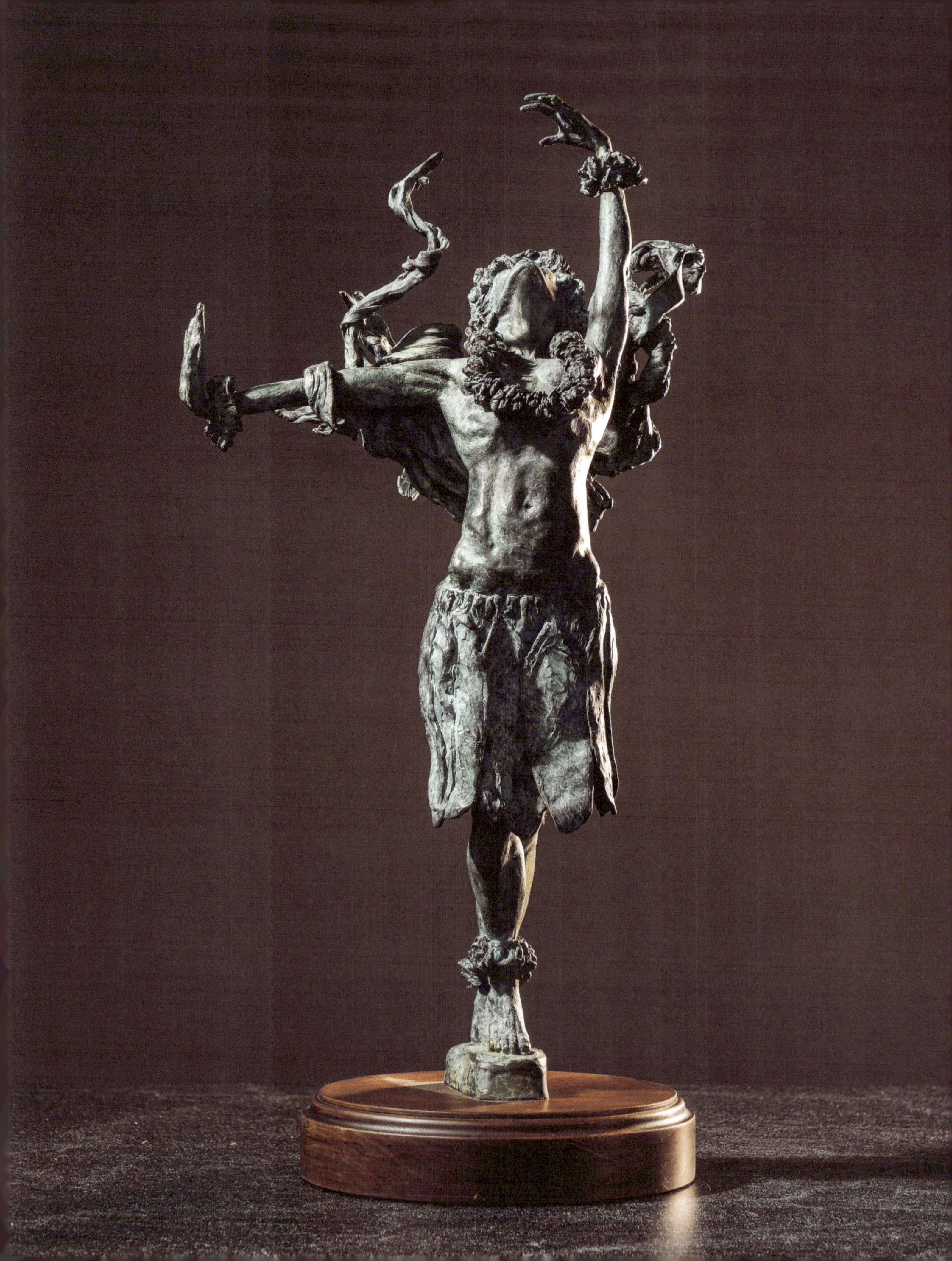

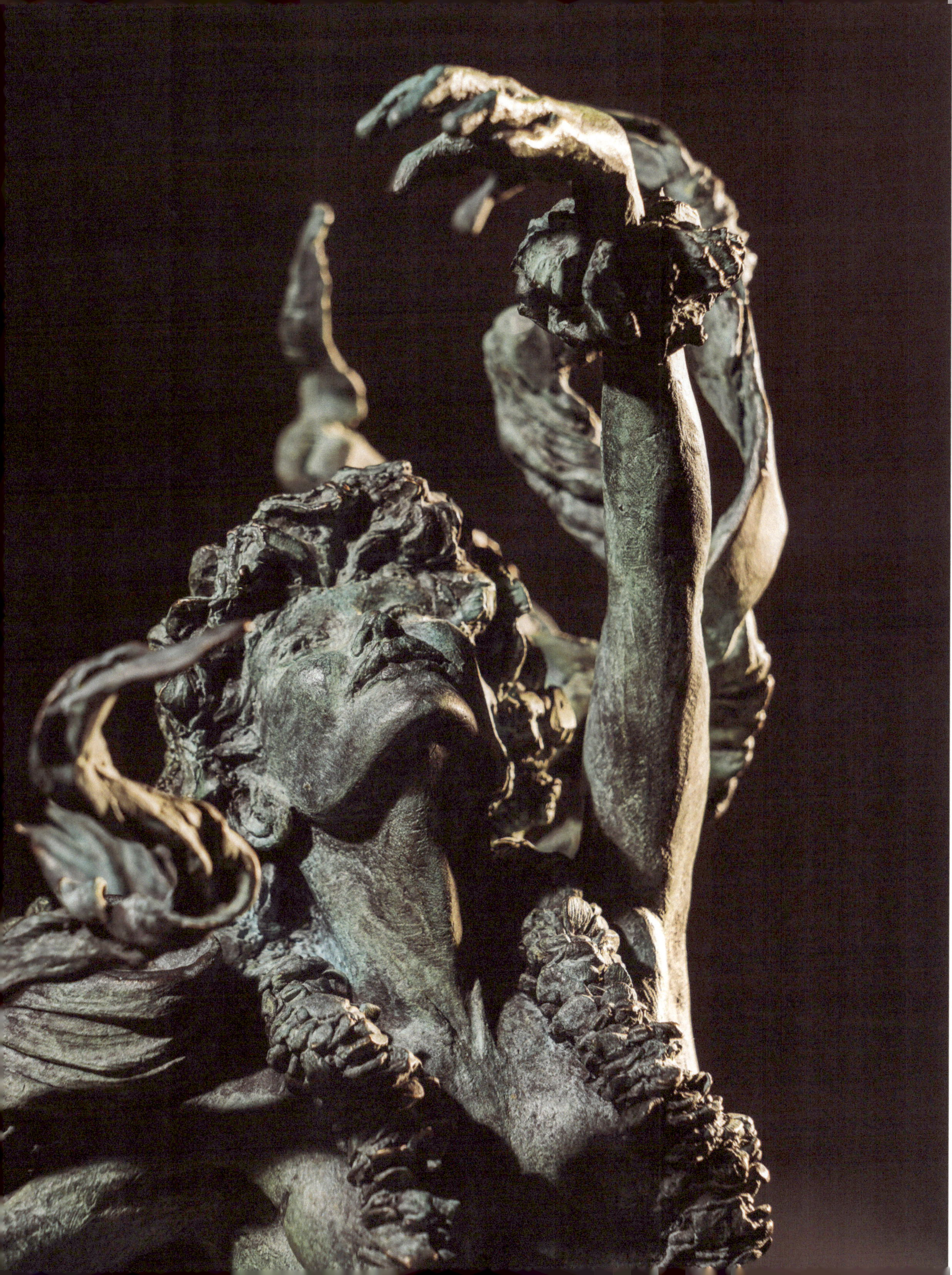

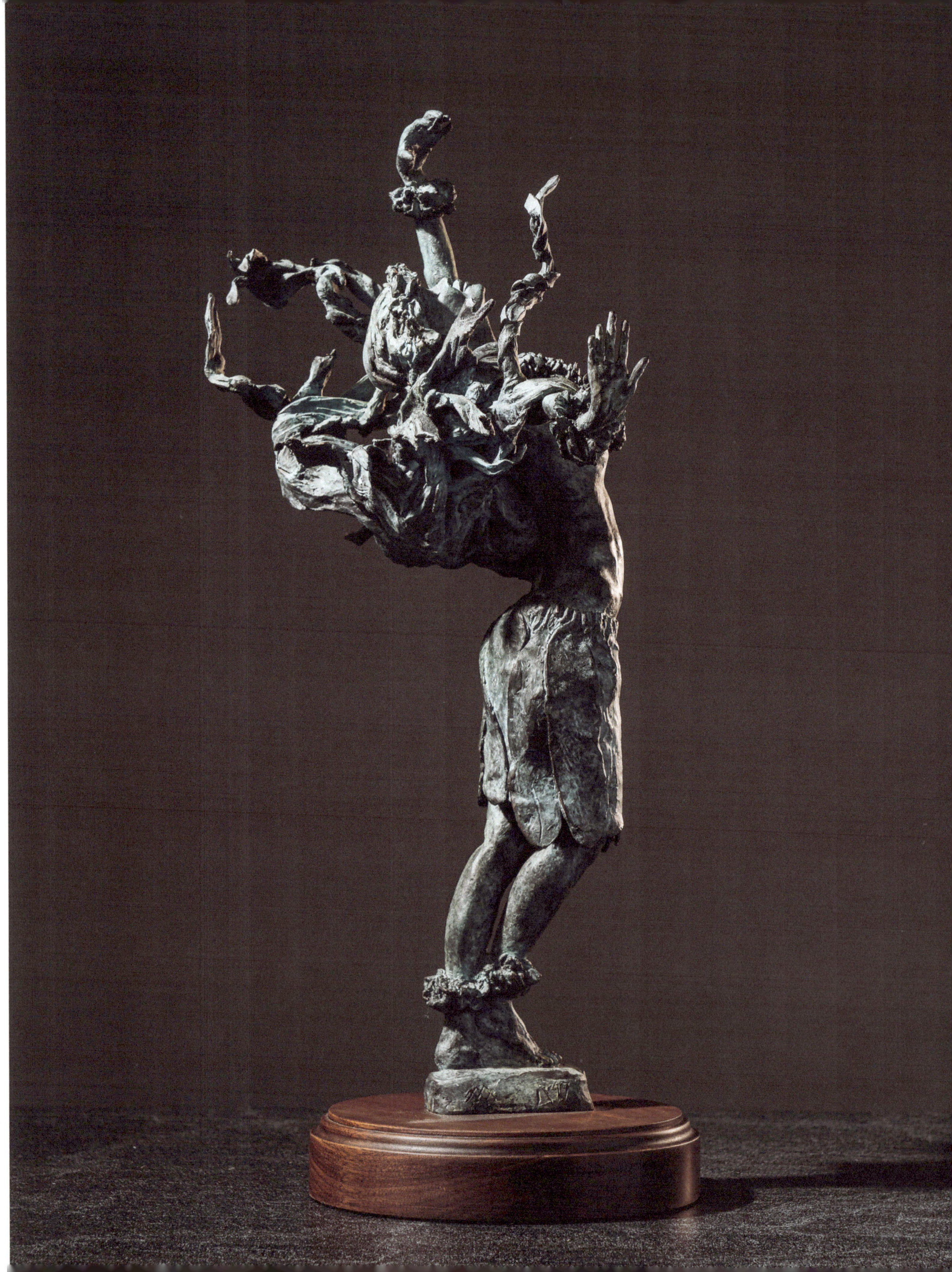

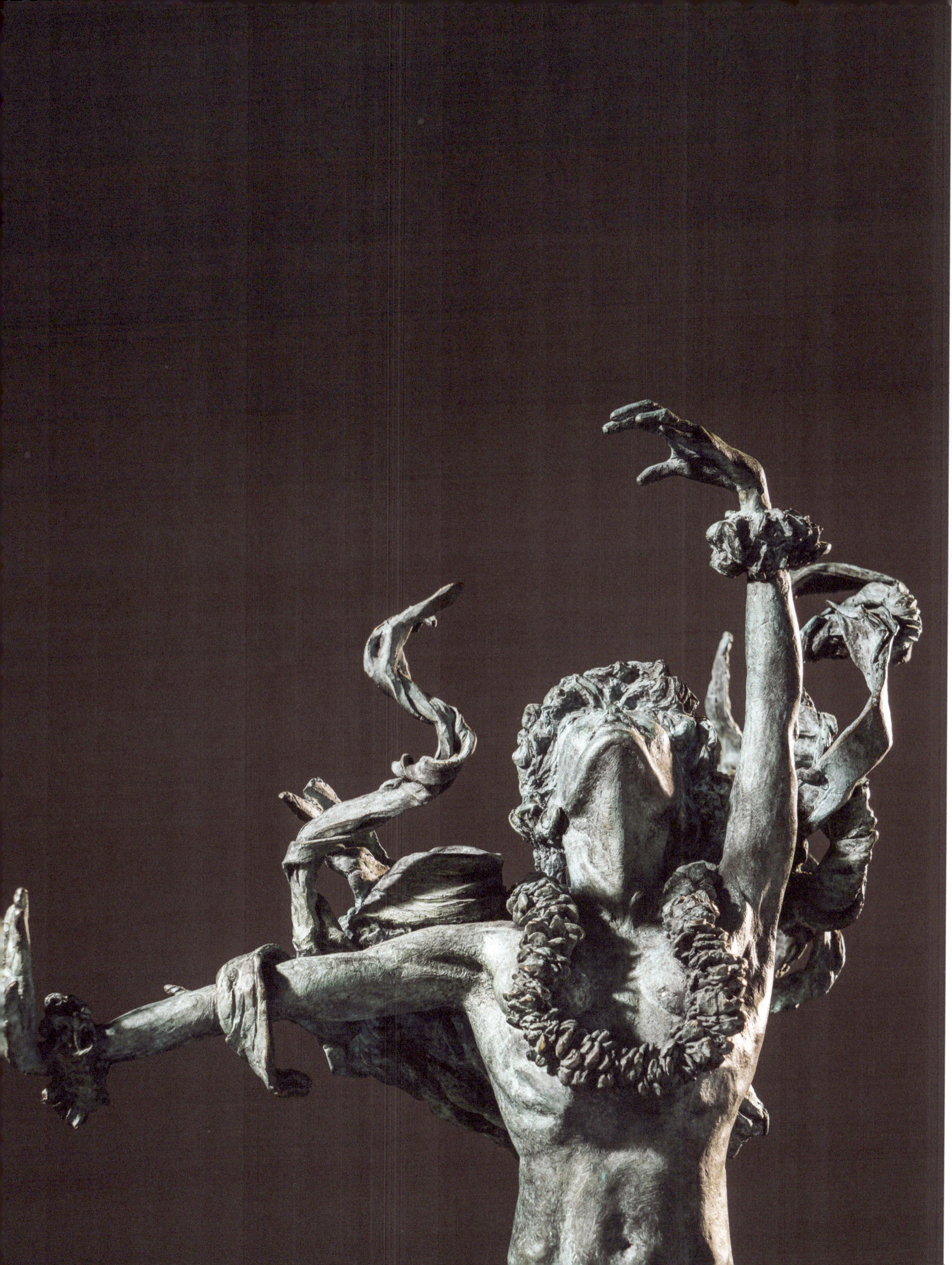

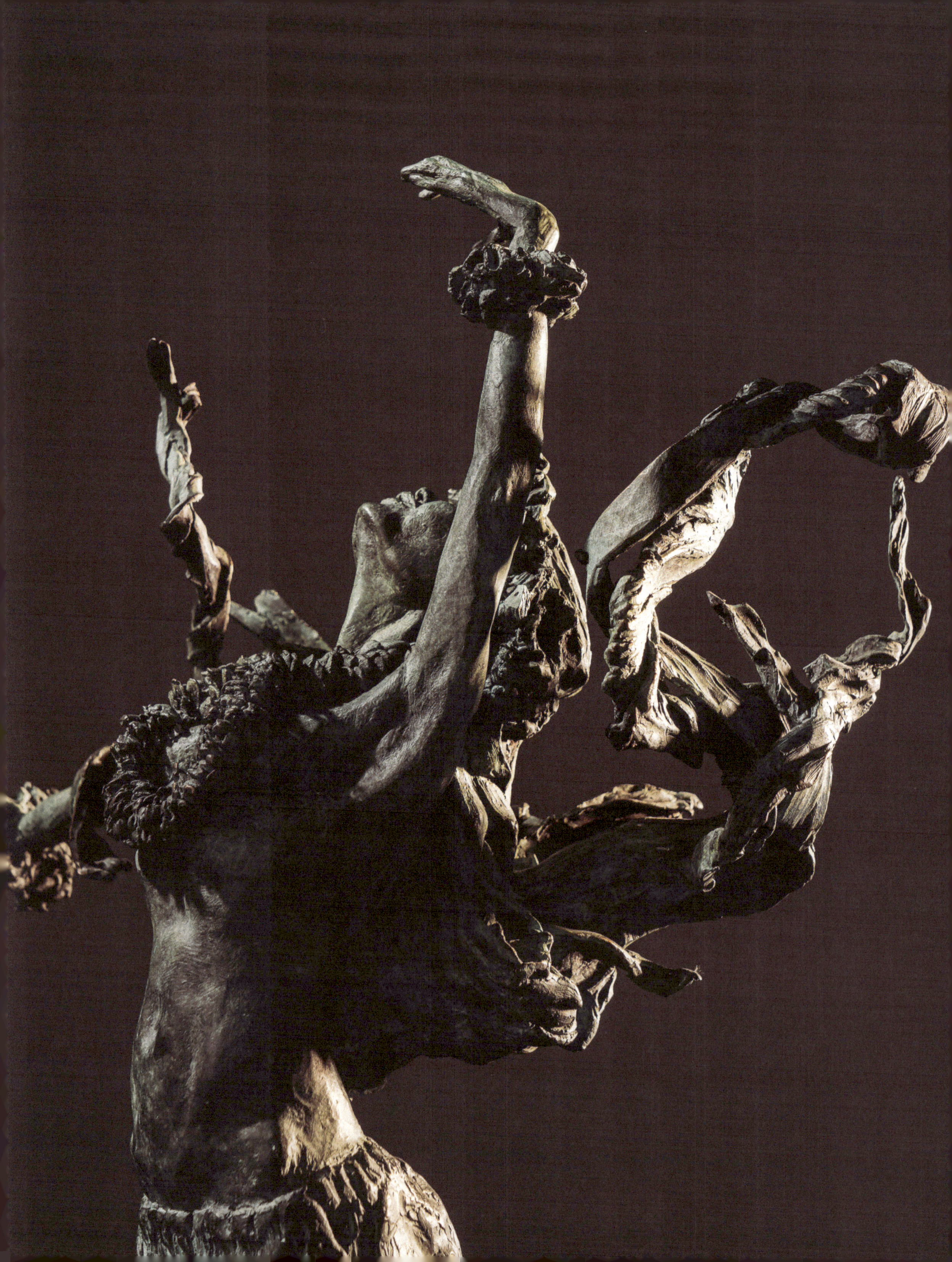

## Eye of the Storm

With Eye of the Storm, I'm posing a question: Does the storm of life have us in its grip, or, at times, are we the source of the storm, generating the chaos around us? I embrace the idea of acting rather than allowing the world to act on me.

Two collectors were drawn to this piece because they live life this way: acting instead of being acted on. One even has a T-shirt that says, "They whispered to her, 'You can't withstand the storm.' She whispered back, 'I am the storm.'"

In Eye of the Storm, I left the figure nude to emphasize that we are at our best when we remain true to who we are. When we know ourselves, what others think about us is irrelevant. That confidence develops as we prove to ourselves again and again that we create our value.

I read somewhere that it's common for animals, employing a kind of sixth sense, to seek shelter against an approaching storm. Buffalo, however, when faced with a storm, don't run away or gather into a protective circle—they charge directly into a storm. When we grasp that struggle fosters growth, we may find ourselves running toward challenges.

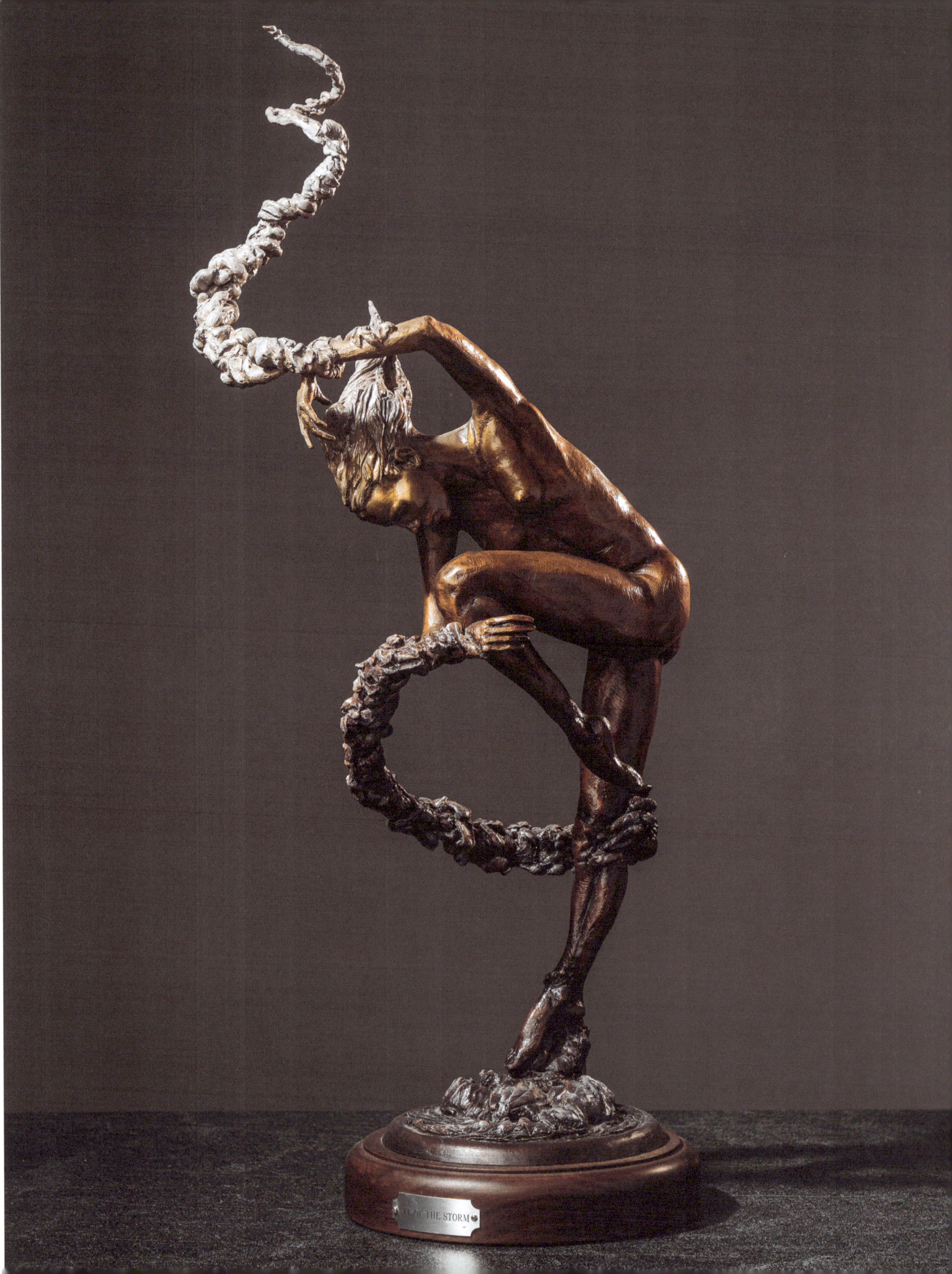
EYE OF THE STORM

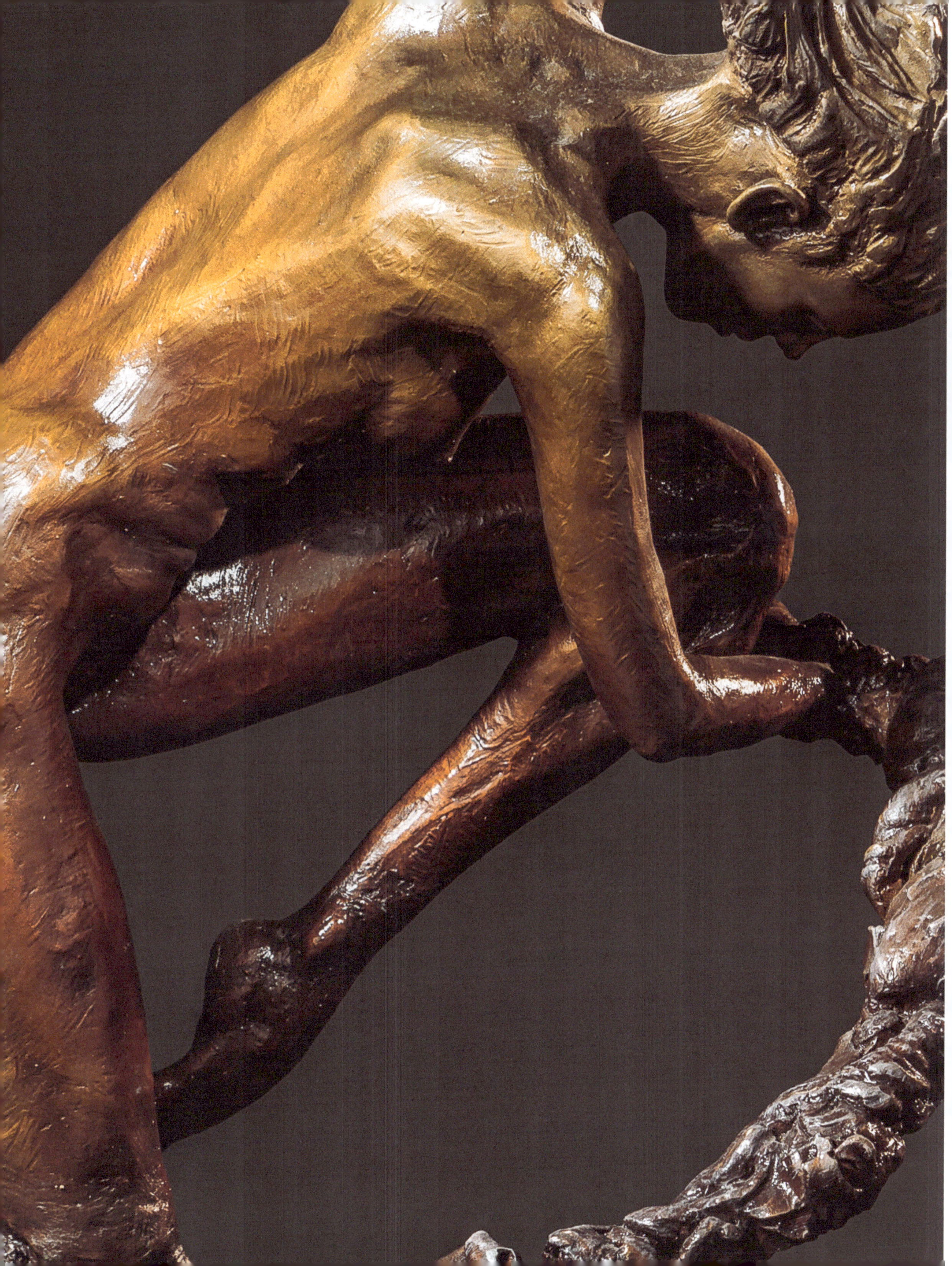

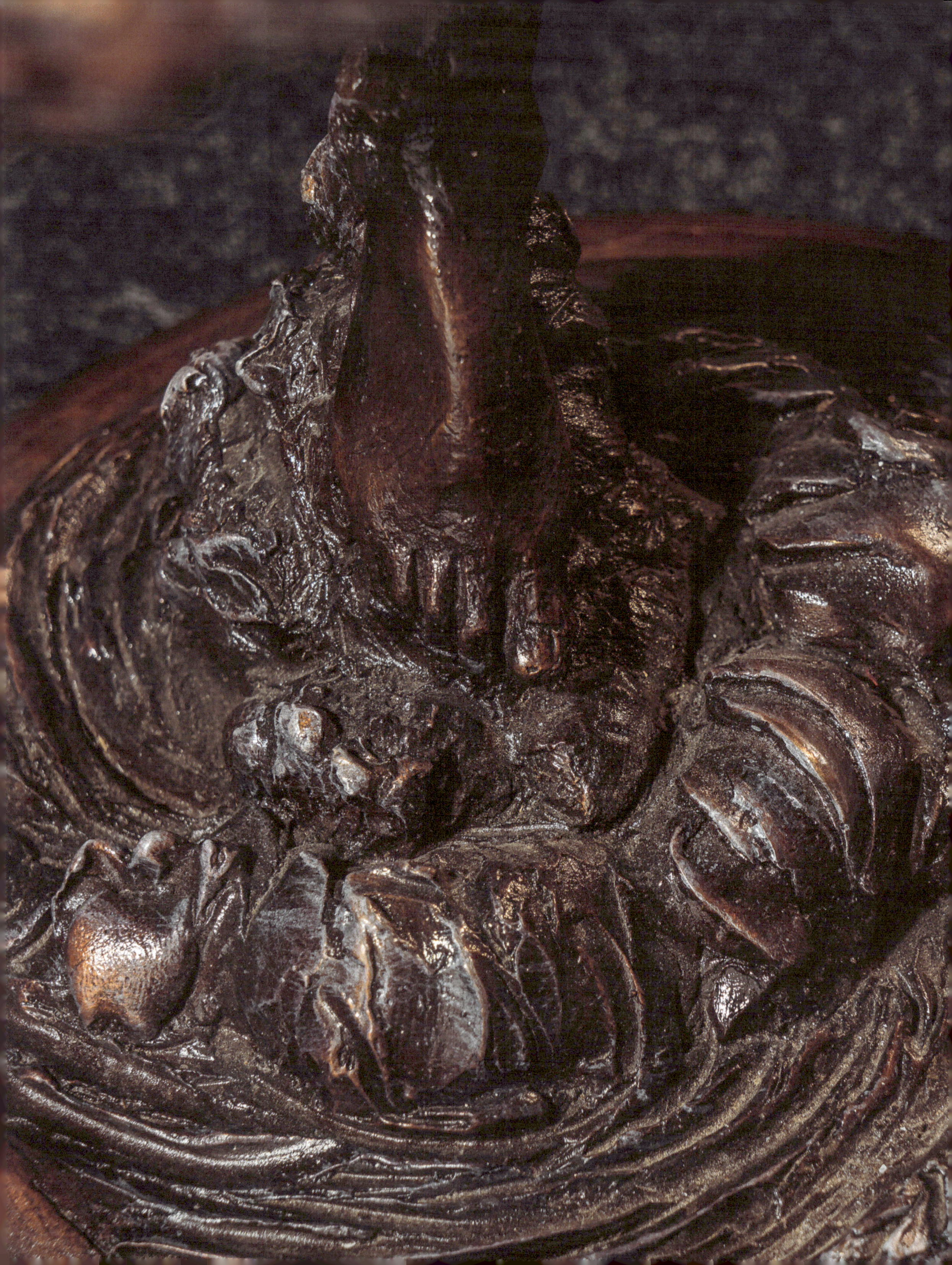

# **Rise**

Why are some people better at handling challenges than others? Rise is inspired by a hero in my community who, at birth, had both legs amputated for medical reasons.

I first became aware of him at a track meet my son participated in. With blade prosthetics, this young man competed—and excelled. So inspiring!

I learned later that his prosthetics caused significant pain, bleeding, and bruising every time he ran, a reality most spectators never saw. Despite the pain, this young athlete had a successful high school and college career, ultimately winning multiple medals in the Paralympic Games.

As far as I know, no one has ever sculpted someone with a physical disability. If that's true (and I hope it isn't), I want to bring awareness to the often-unseen heroes who surround us. In sculpting this piece, I didn't draw on any attributes from this young man, attempting, instead, to create something more universal.

The chains that extend along the base act as a key element in this sculpture, each link made individually. What I haven't distinguished is if the runner breaks the chains or if the chains reach out to restrain him. This ambiguity, I hope, asks a deeper question: Is it our strength that allows us to overcome adversity, or does adversity strengthen us?

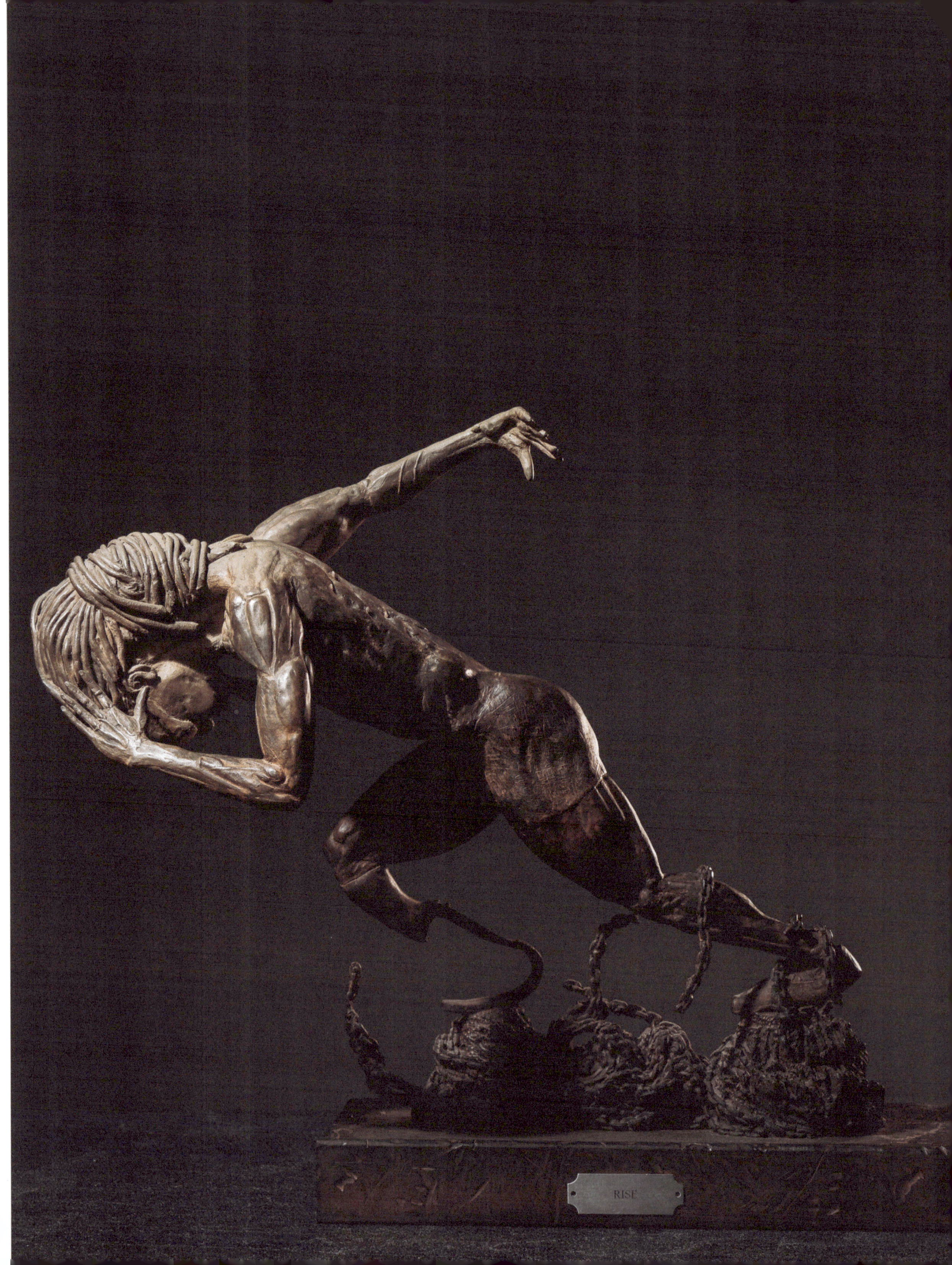
RISE

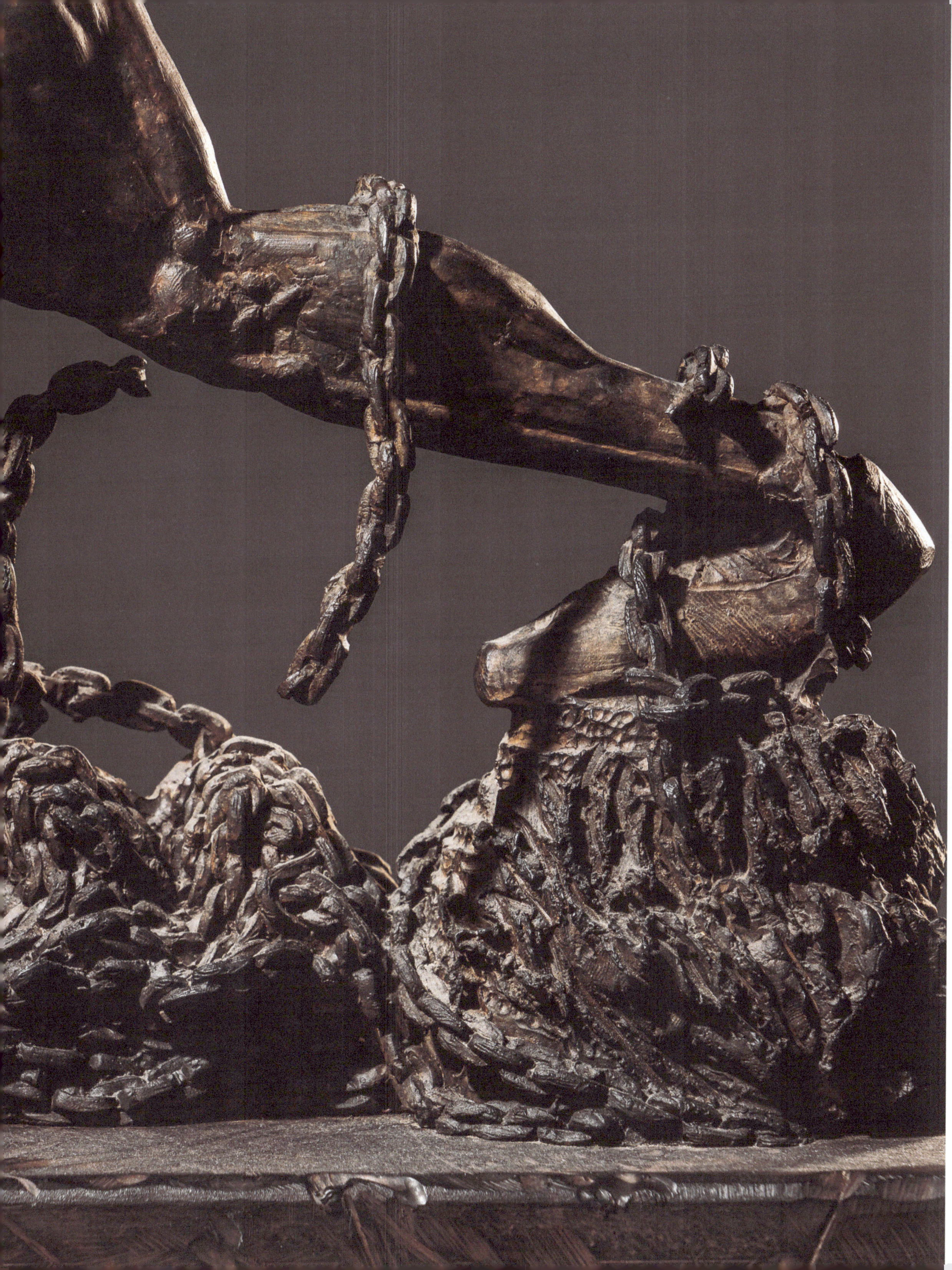

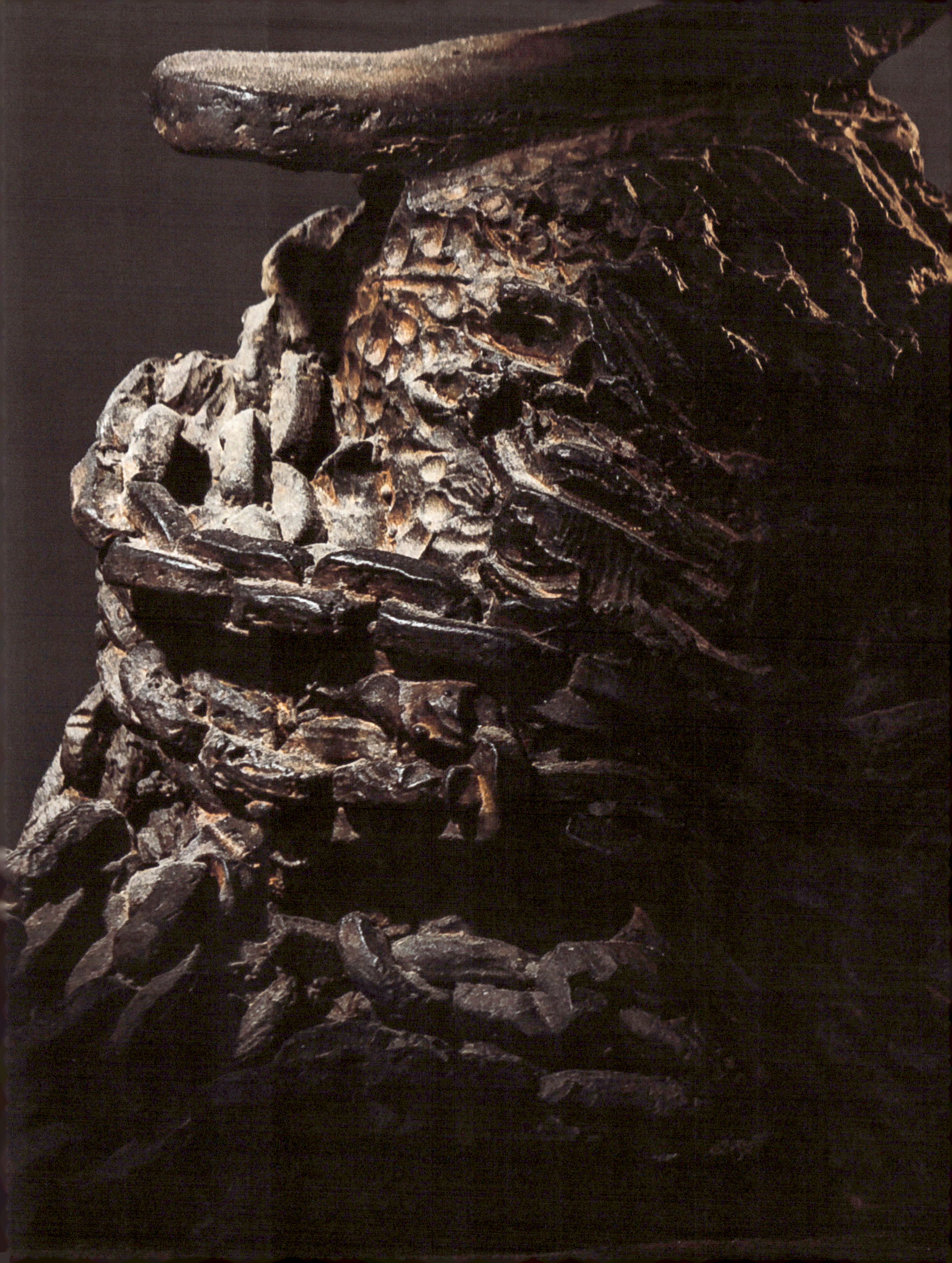

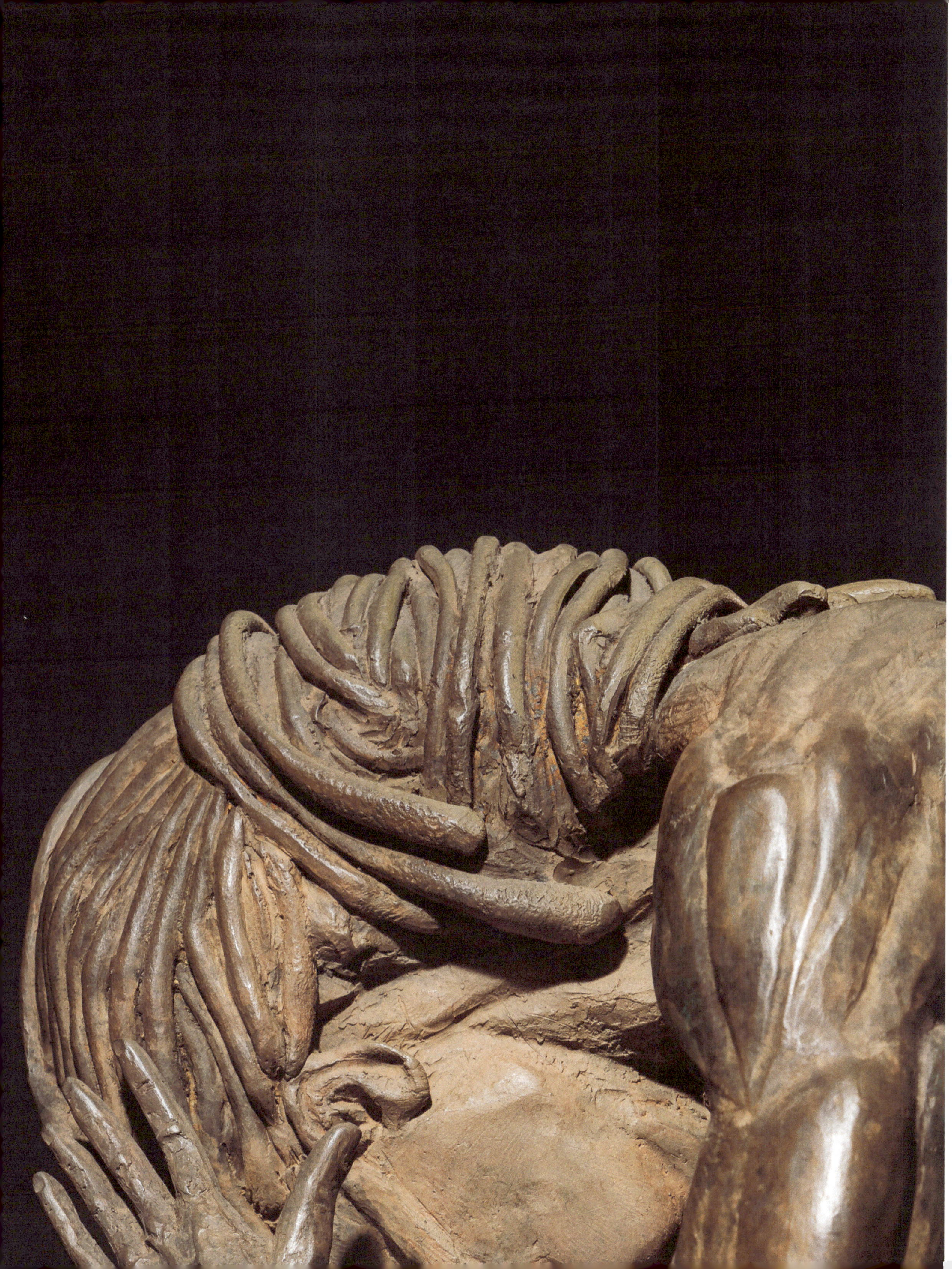

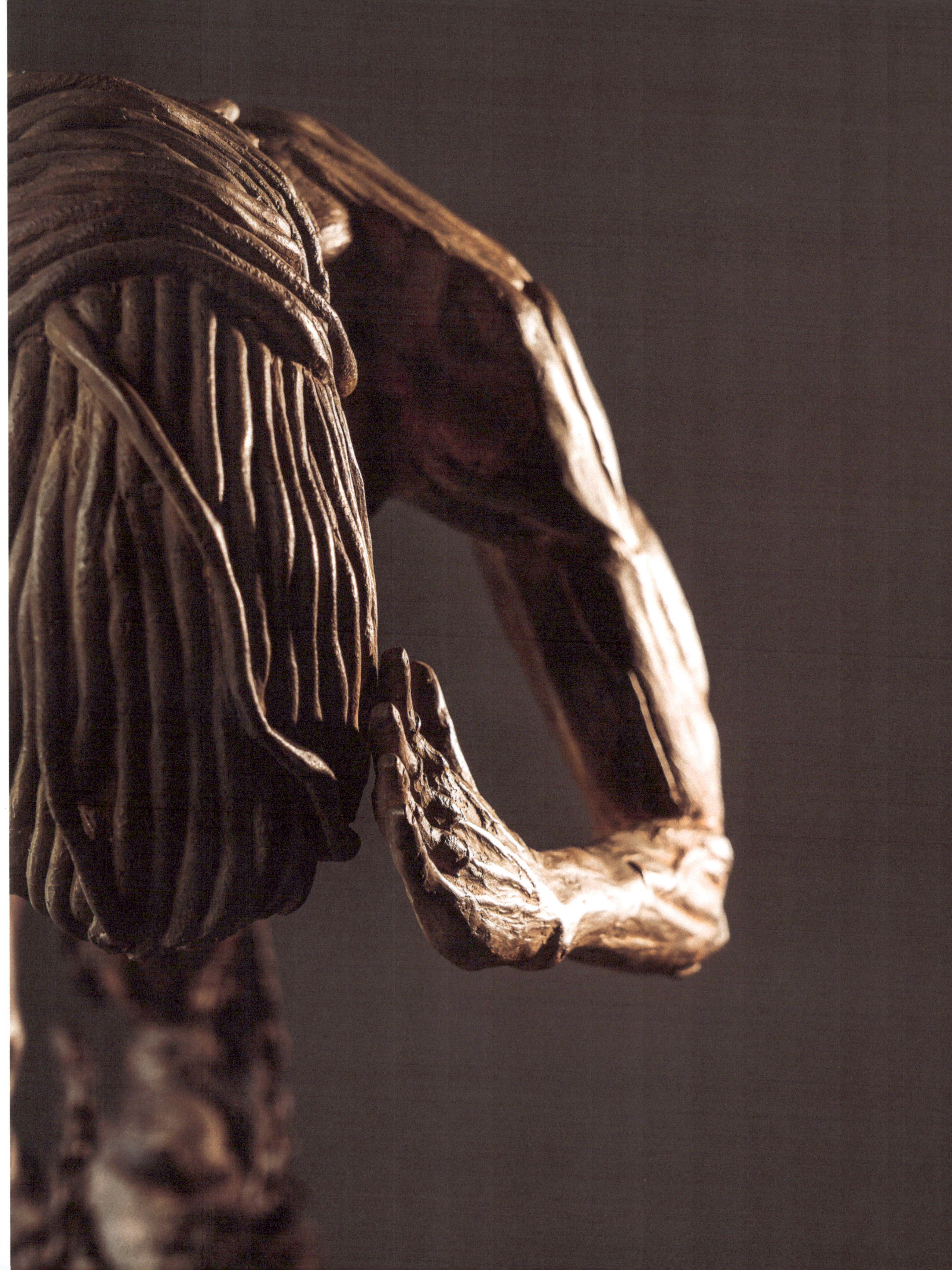

# Hemeroscopium

Hemeroscopium is an allusion to a place that exists only in our minds, in our senses, that is ever-changing and mutable but nonetheless real.

When confronted with something seemingly incomprehensible, we often fail to understand because we focus on explanations from our own individual perspectives and experiences. We want the complicated world we inhabit to make sense, and so we tell ourselves stories to fill the gaps. We become so convinced of our own explanations that we wonder how others can hold views contrary to our own.

A purposeful break to emphasize incompleteness interrupts this sculpture's story. That void honors the idea that there's beauty in not knowing everything and an opportunity to bridge that gap through learning and understanding if we're open and willing to learn from each other.

The moment we dig in and ignore the world's diversity is the moment we deny ourselves progression.

Hemeroscopium provides the secret to keeping our minds open and curious. Though this sculpture is of a mermaid, a creature that doesn't exist, perhaps we can agree that something fictitious can open our minds to the prospect that we don't know everything.

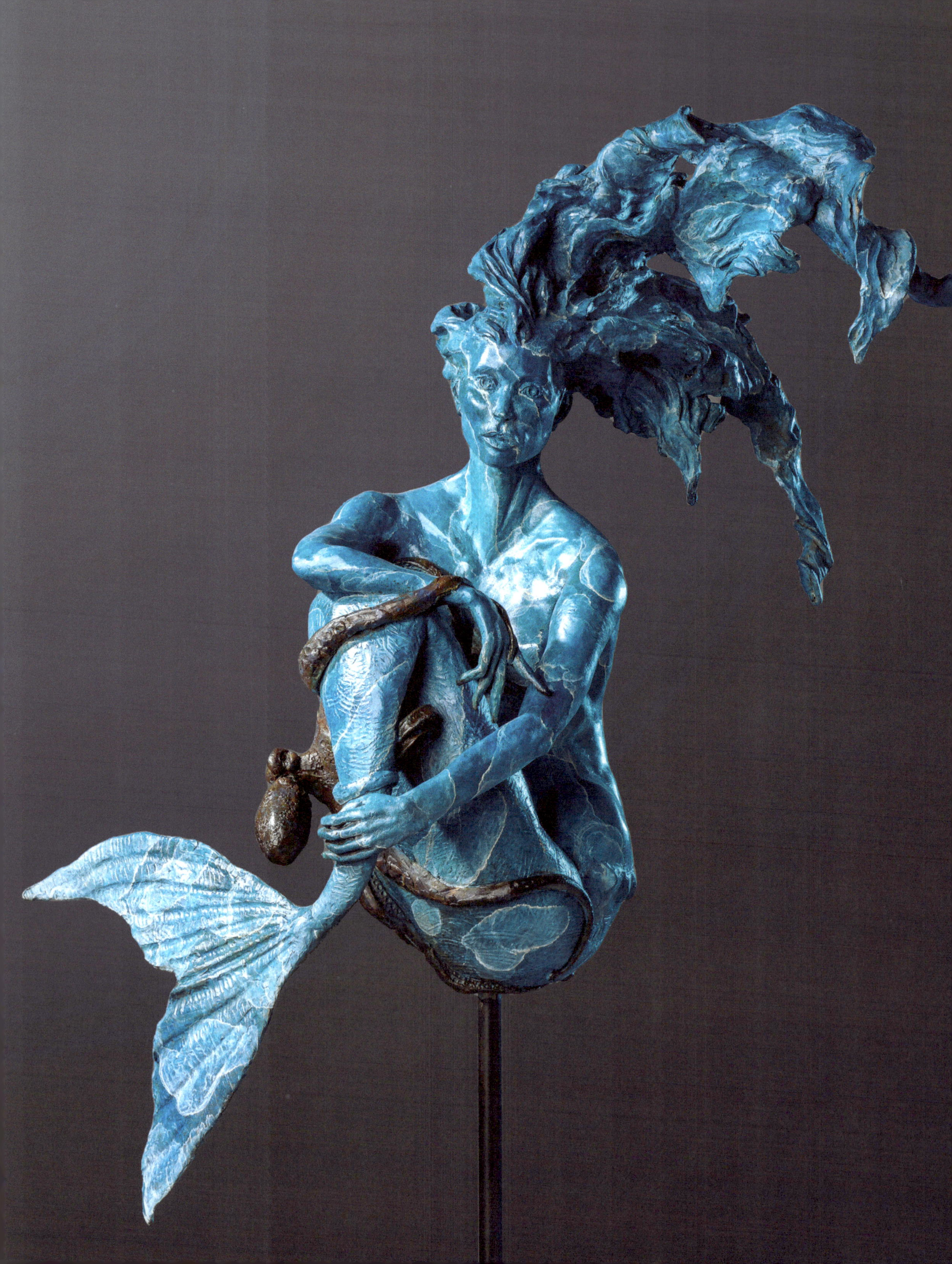

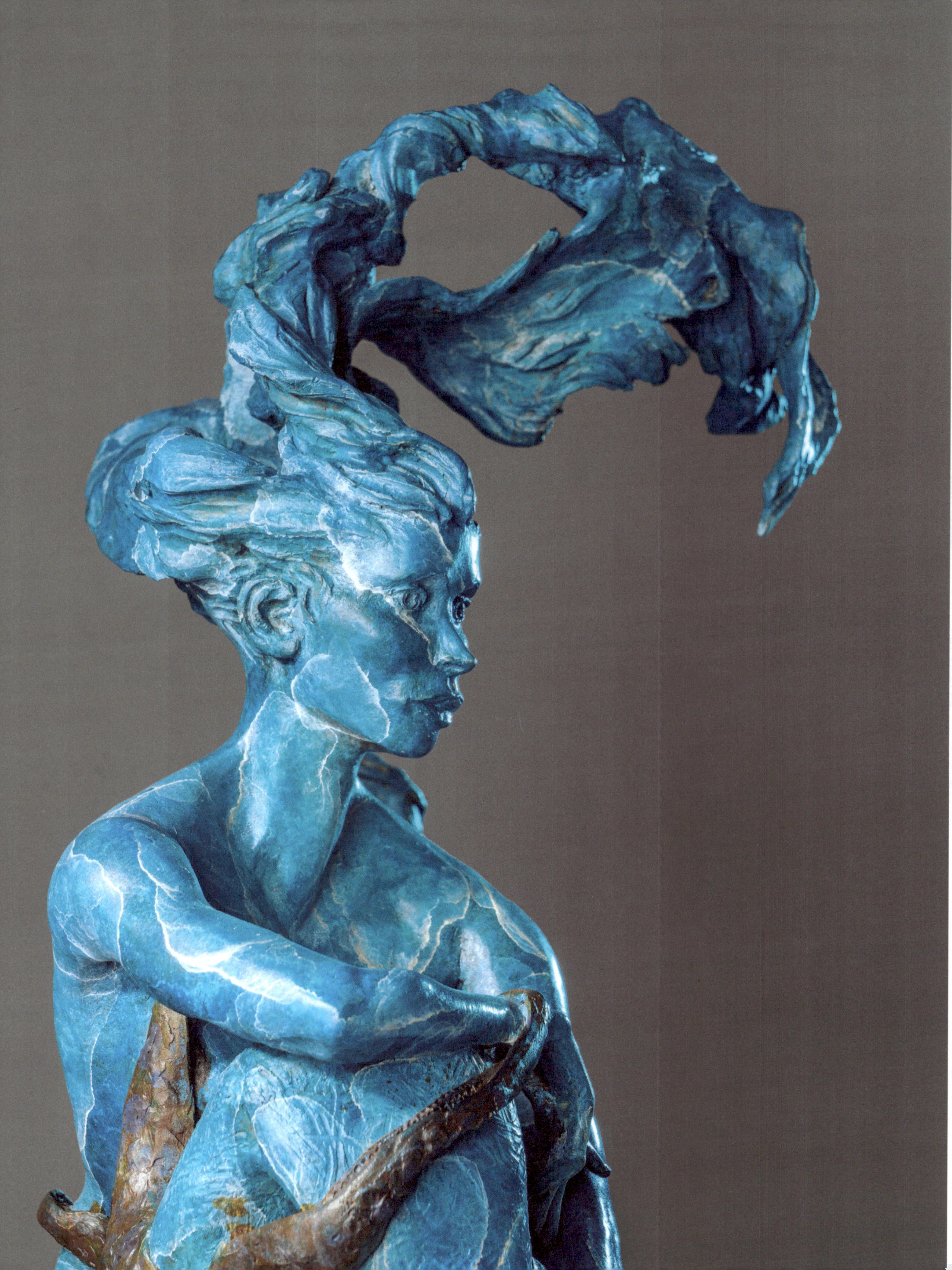

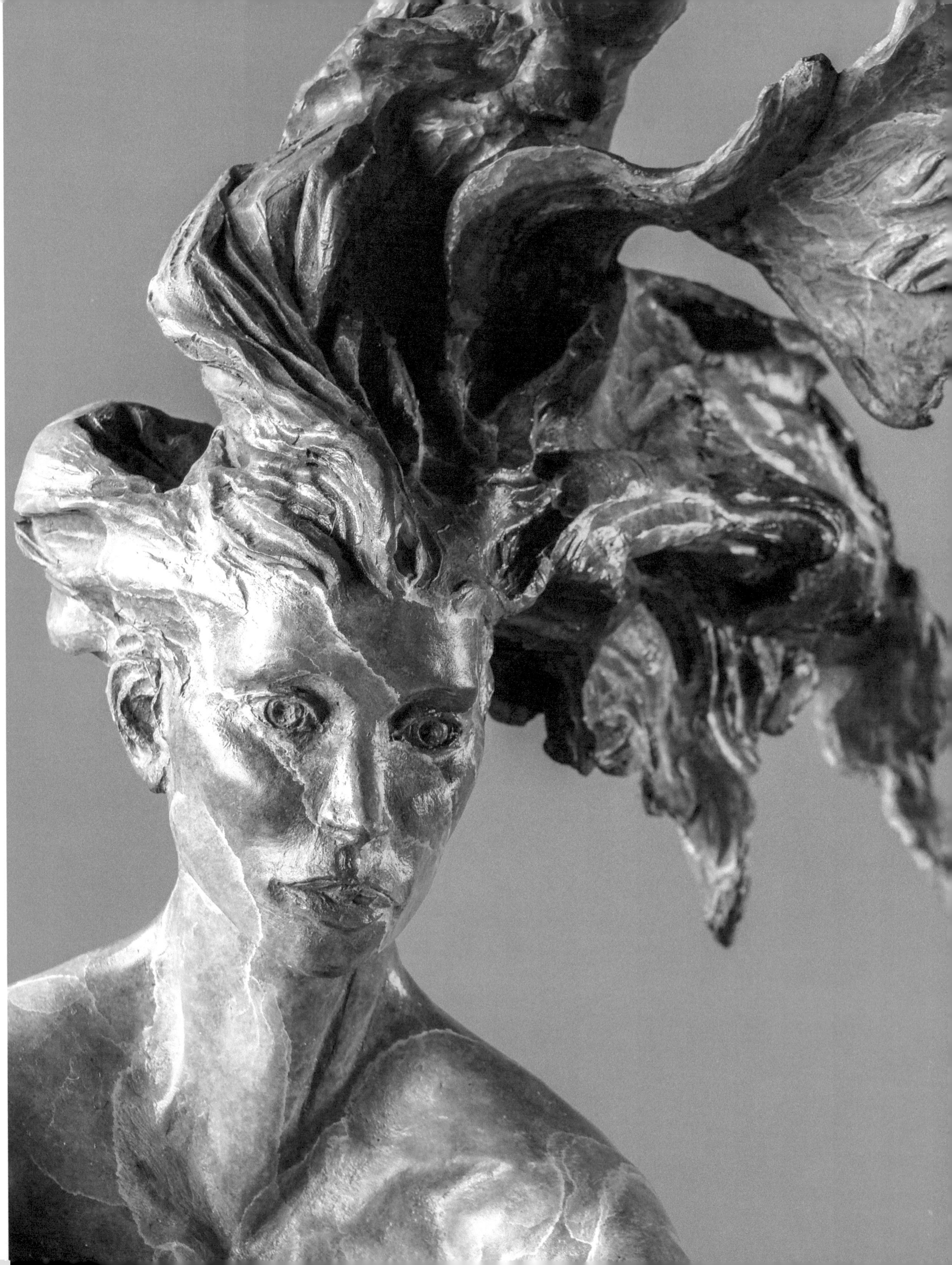

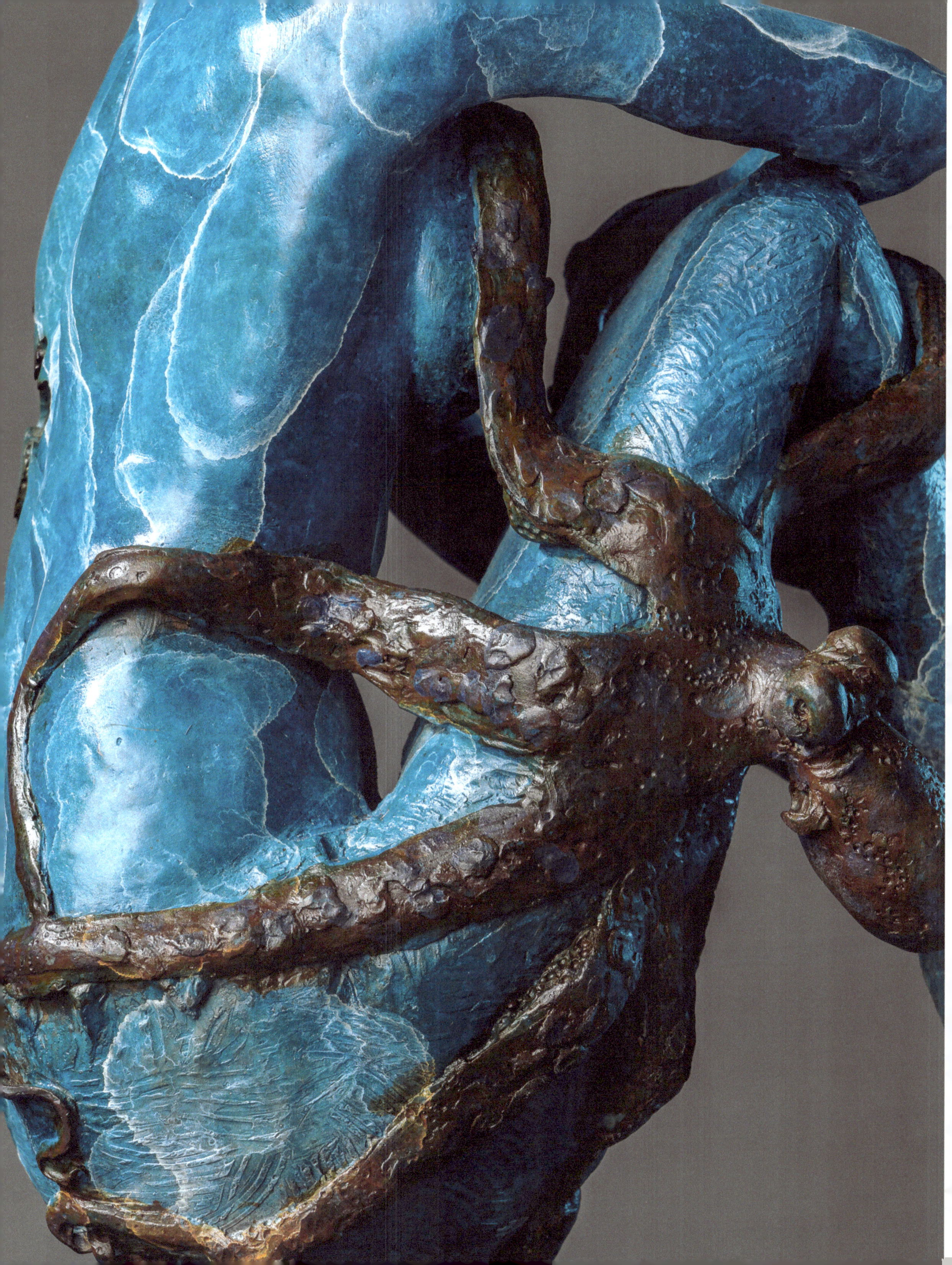

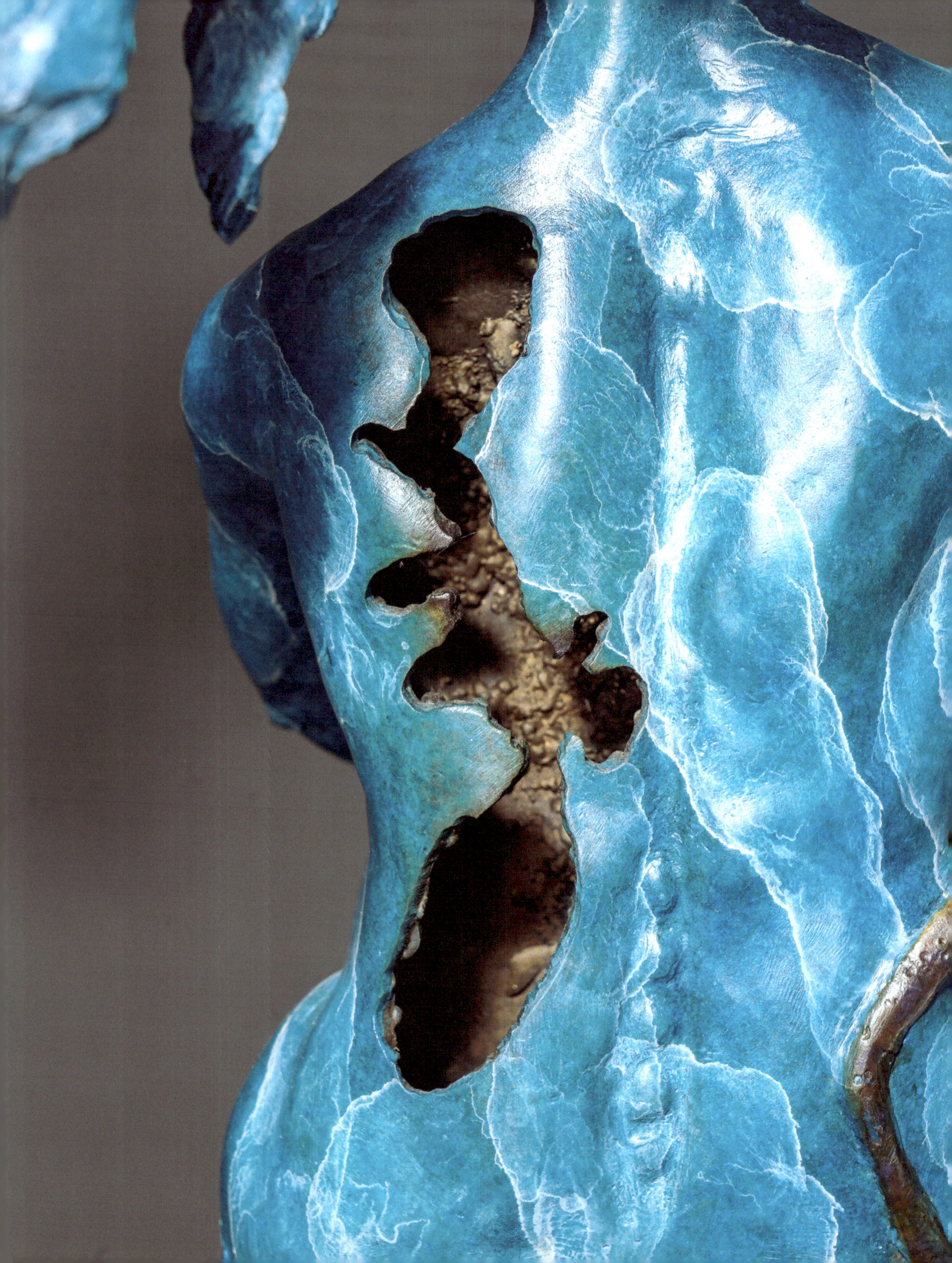

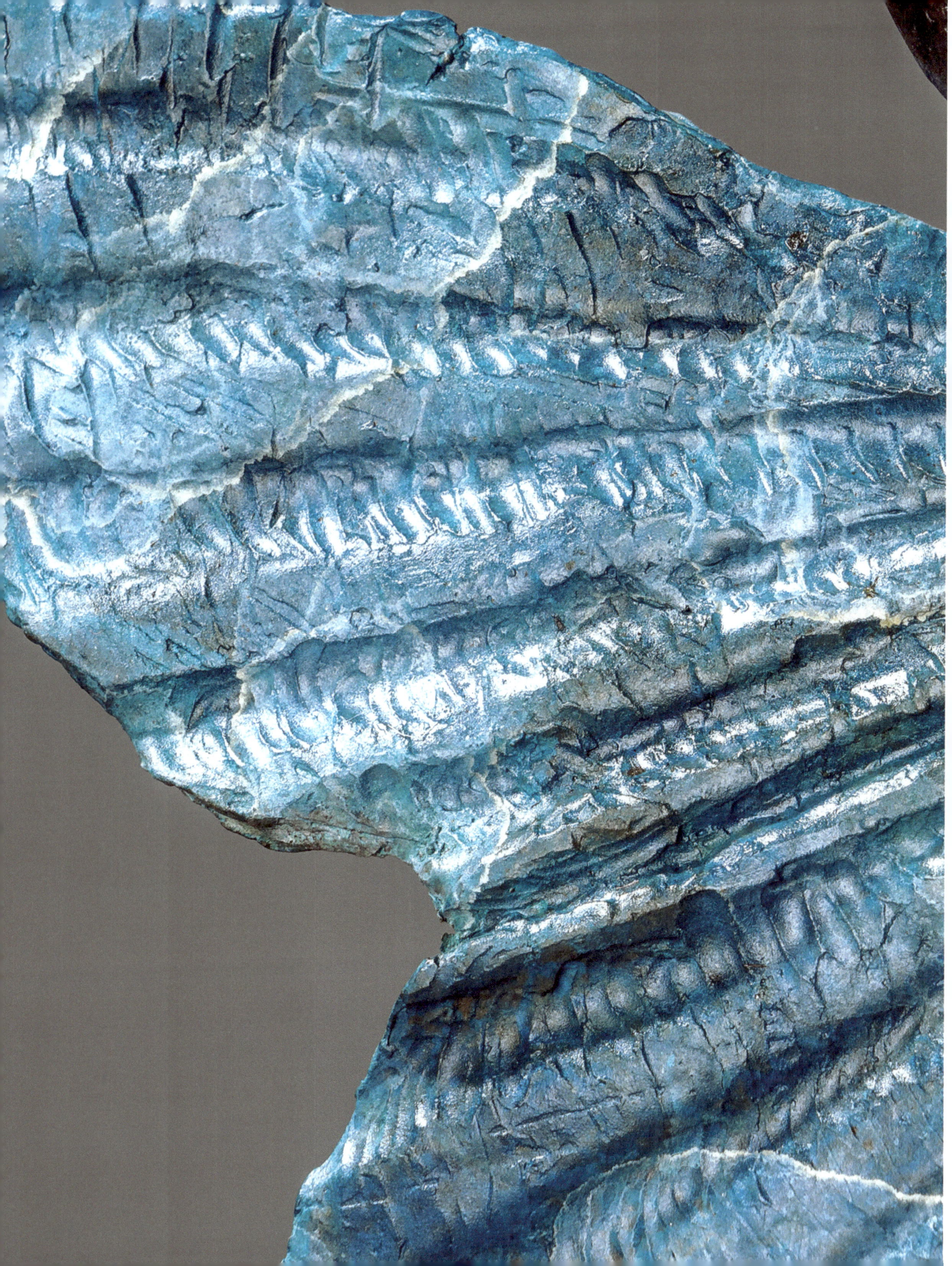

# Refinement

I've come to see how the sculpting process is a lot like life: you begin with raw, shapeless clay teeming with unknown potential. Add more clay, and take some away. Combined energy and work through heat and pressure effect even more change.

Incrementally, an idea morphs into a form, a form exudes an emotion; an emotion conveys a story that connects with someone. Over time, organization and beauty emerge from the abstract, and order emerges from cacophony. Nothing becomes something.

Most often, my sculptures are complete disasters. Aren't we sometimes the same? Life is a process, and, fortunately, there's no end to our development. Potential equals change. We must live life so that we're constantly becoming. We change what we don't like. We become what we like. The choice is ours. Refinement.

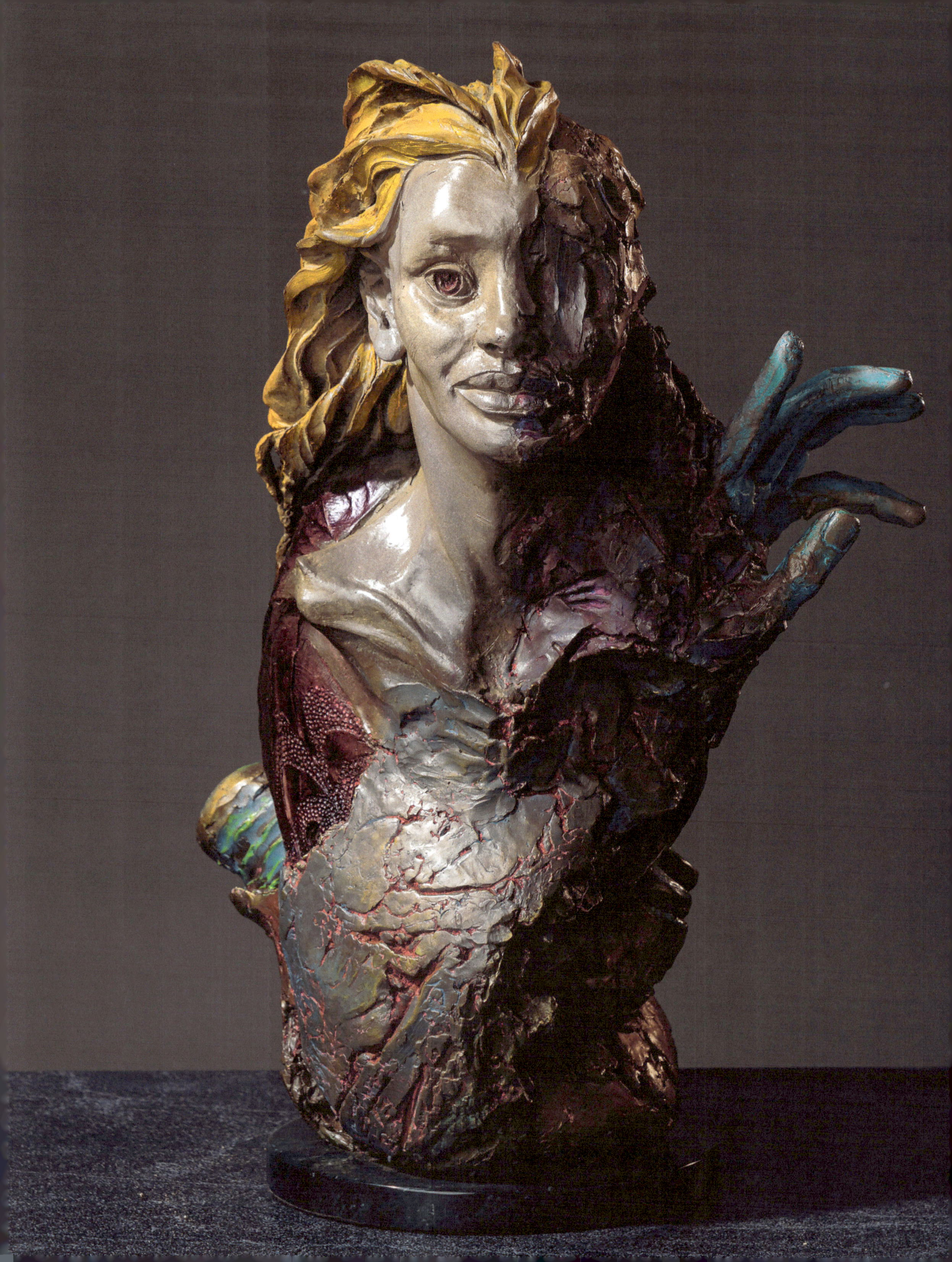

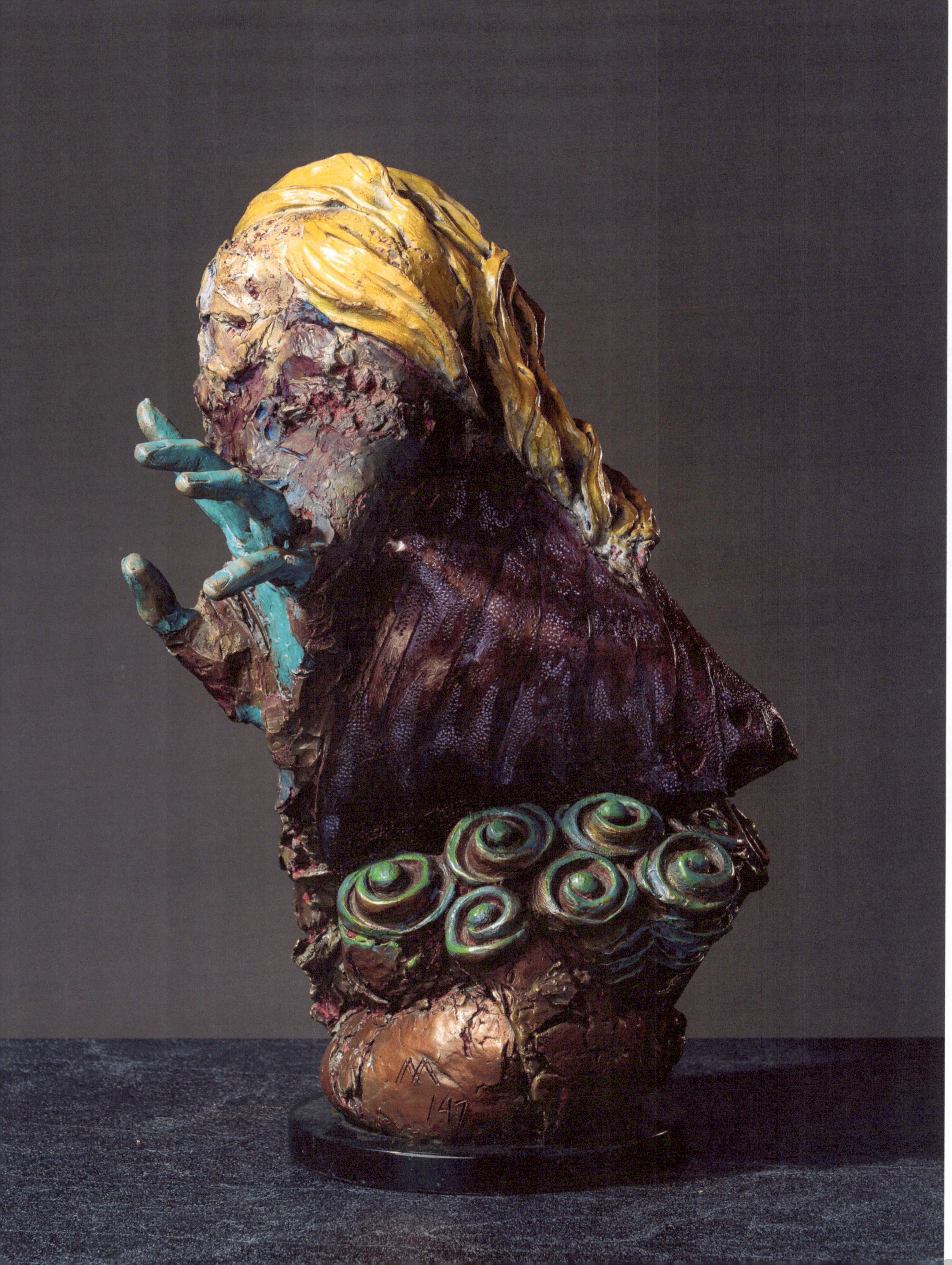

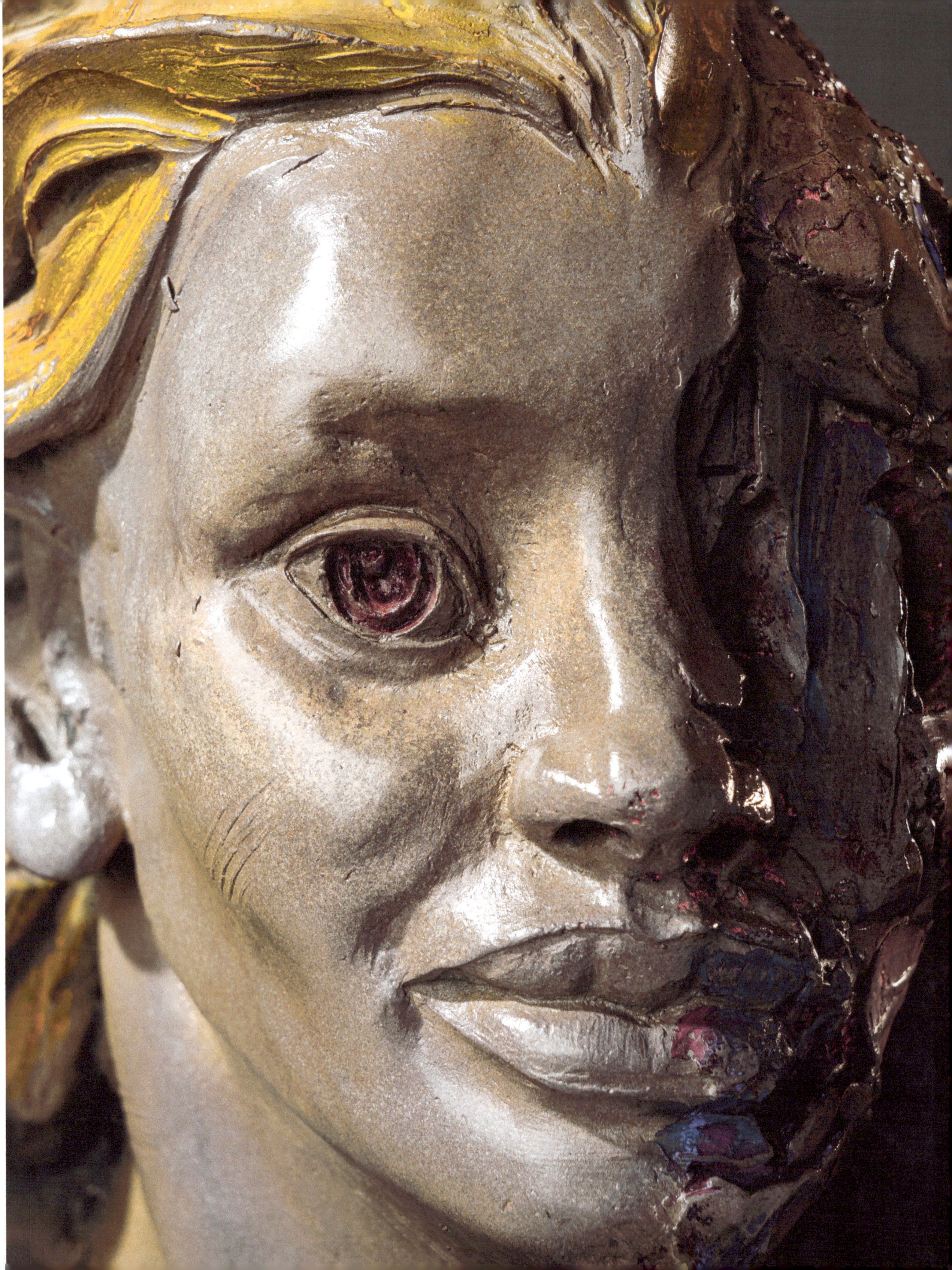

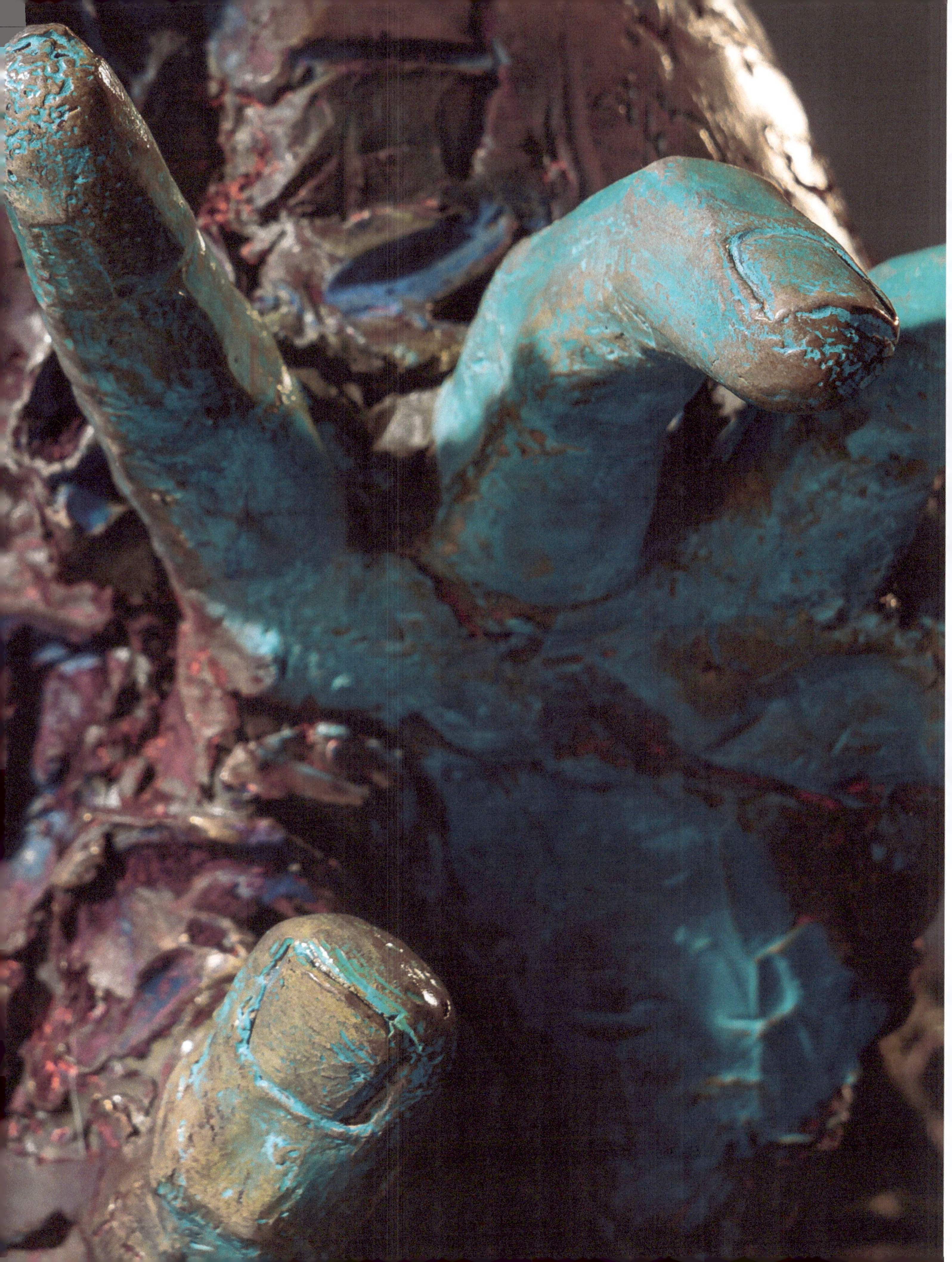

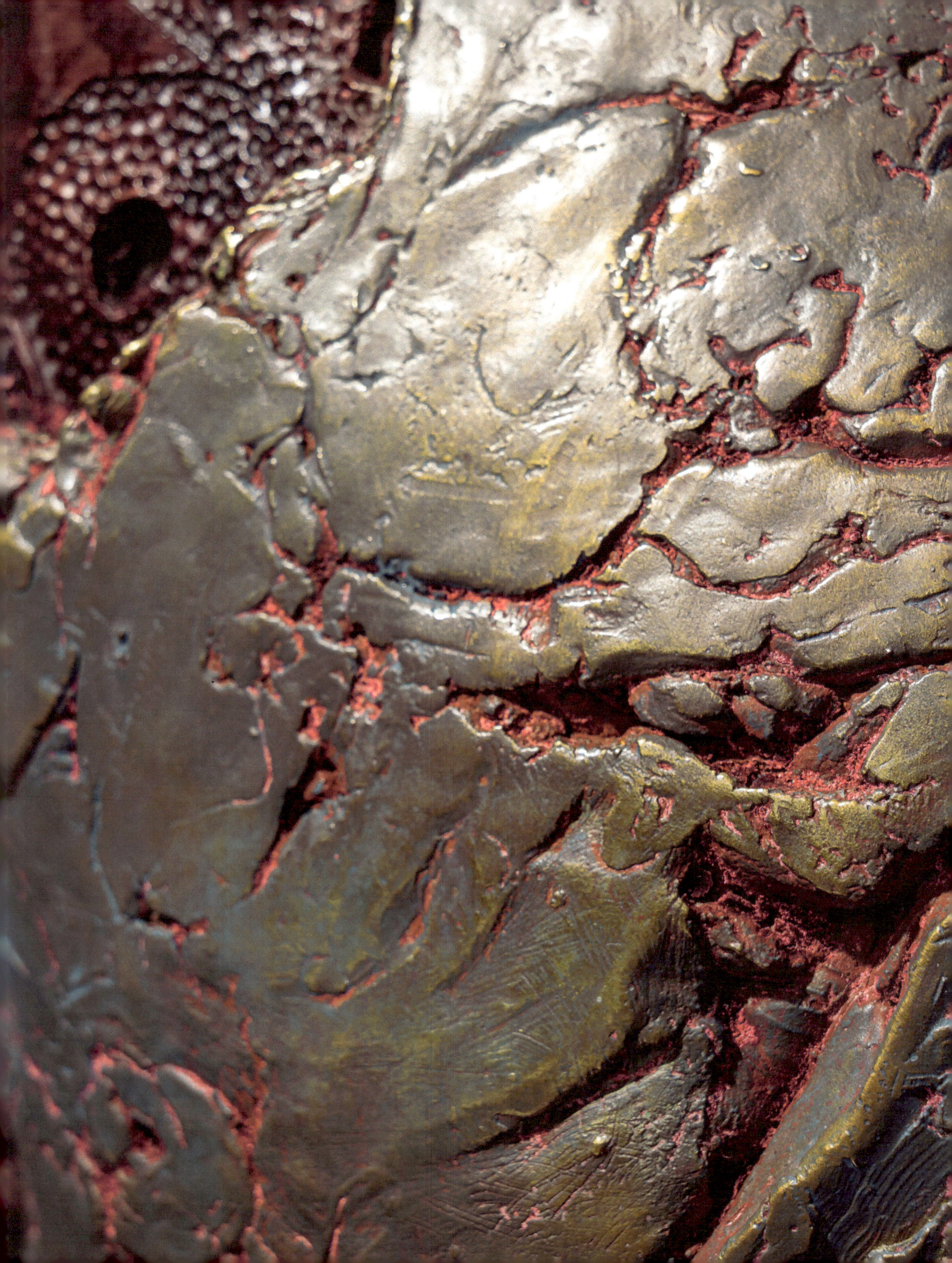

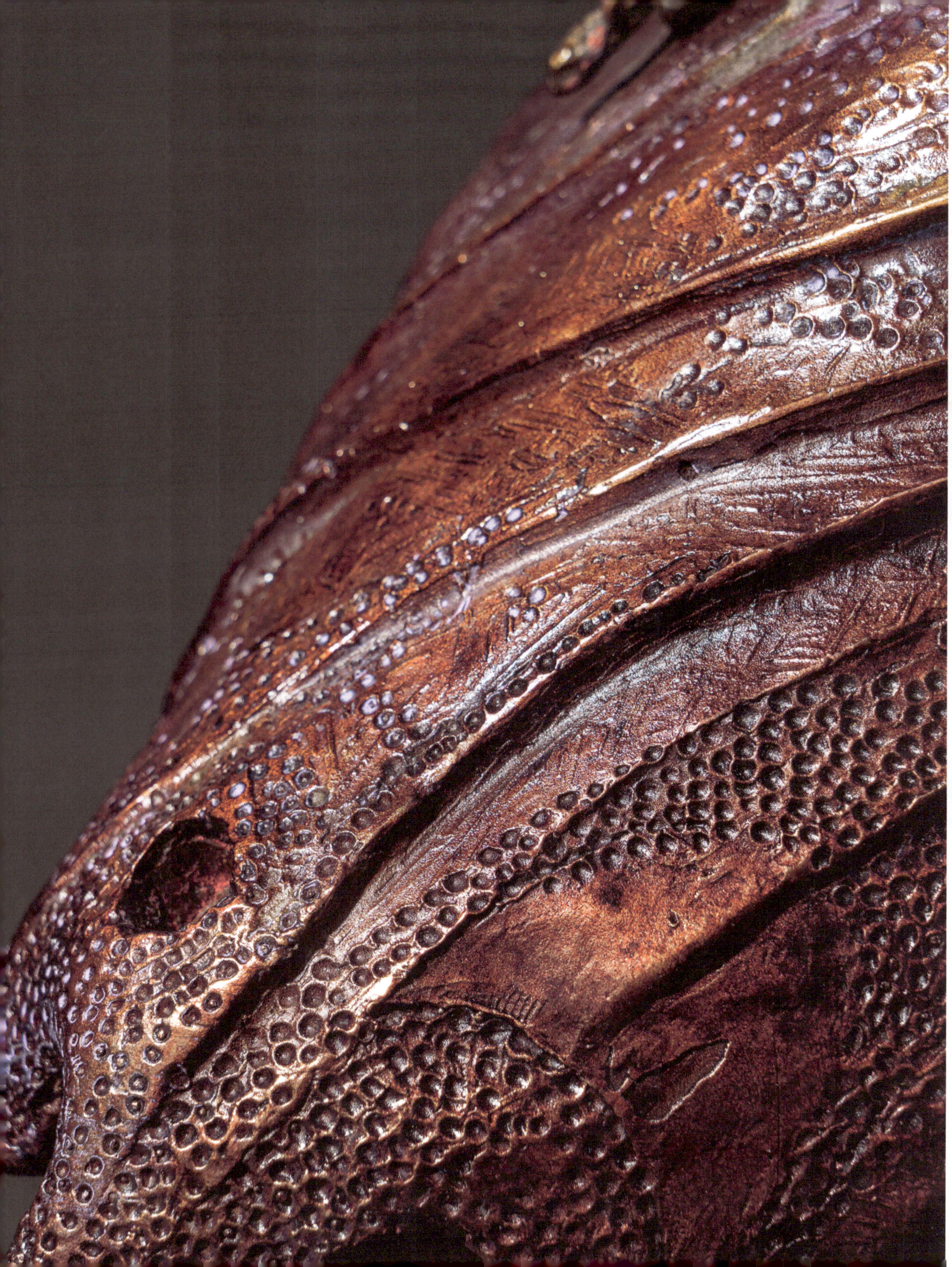

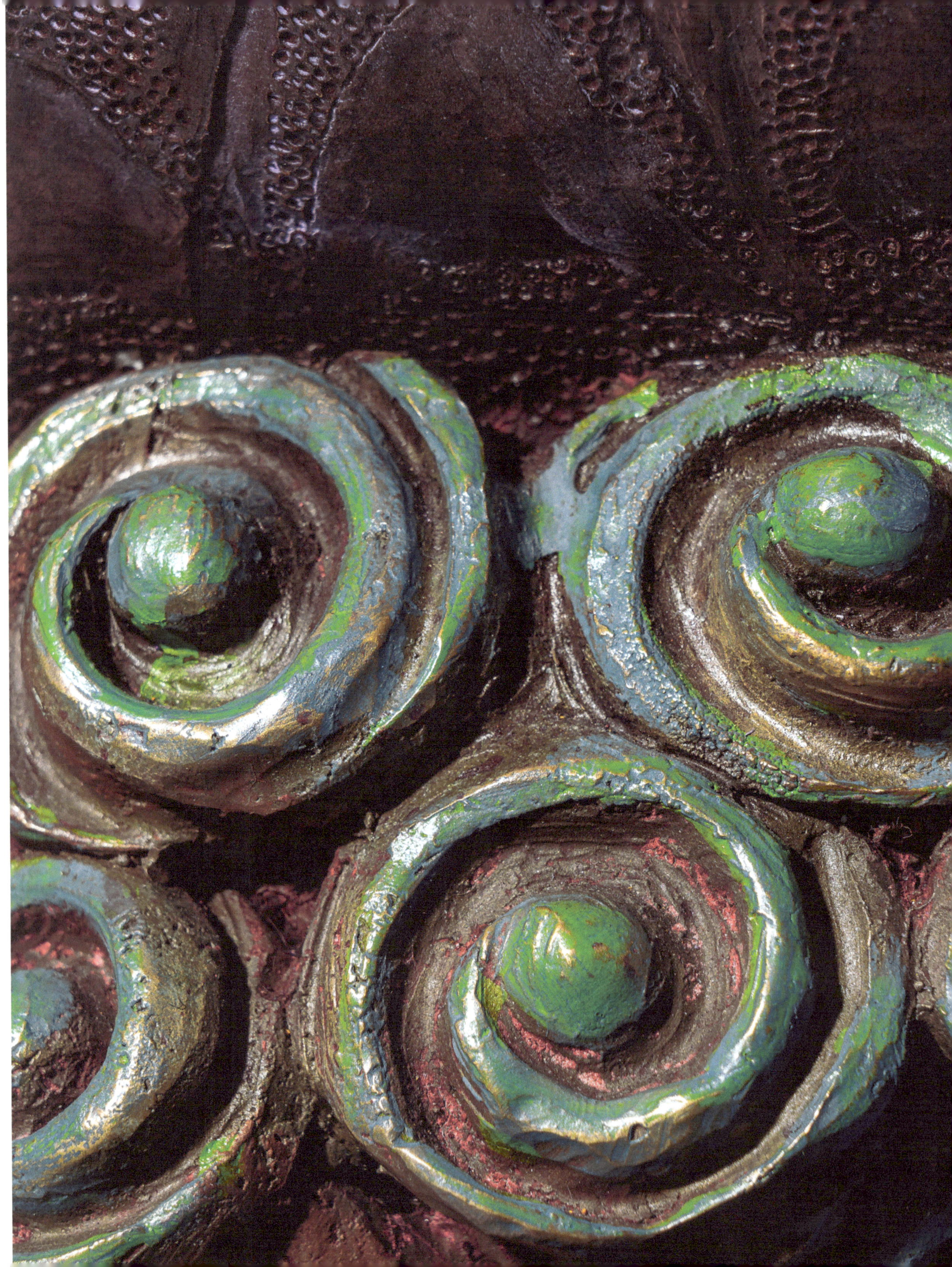

# Birth of a Mermaid

Birth of a Mermaid is the final piece of my Ocean Tides Series, a series that embodies my love of the ocean and attempts to connect with others who share my love. In my initial concept of this piece, I imagined a mermaid emerging from a shell and experiencing the world for the first time. I wanted to connect the image of the mermaid with the life cycles of hermit crabs and, further, to the cycles of desire and action in our own lives. Let me explain:

Hermit crabs fascinate me because they use their shells for protection, yet they can't make their own shells. Instead, they must fight to acquire new shells as they outgrow their old ones, ideally searching for one that will continue to fit as they grow. How interesting if, just like the hermit crab, we had an outward manifestation of our own personal growth.

But protection isn't the only reason for these shells. At times, it's been observed that hermit crabs change shells simply because they find a shell that's more beautiful. In the human realm, there's a psychological term for this: The mimetic theory of desire. Simply, this theory asserts that we don't naturally know what will make us happy, so we mimic what others do to find happiness. There's a lesson here: Do we rely on others for our happiness, or do we trust ourselves and our abilities?

There's no guarantee that mindlessly mimicking others or acquiring what others possess will secure lasting happiness. We can do better than the hermit crab. We can make our own shells and customize them to our needs and preferences. With confidence, we can make room to expand and grow in the world we create.

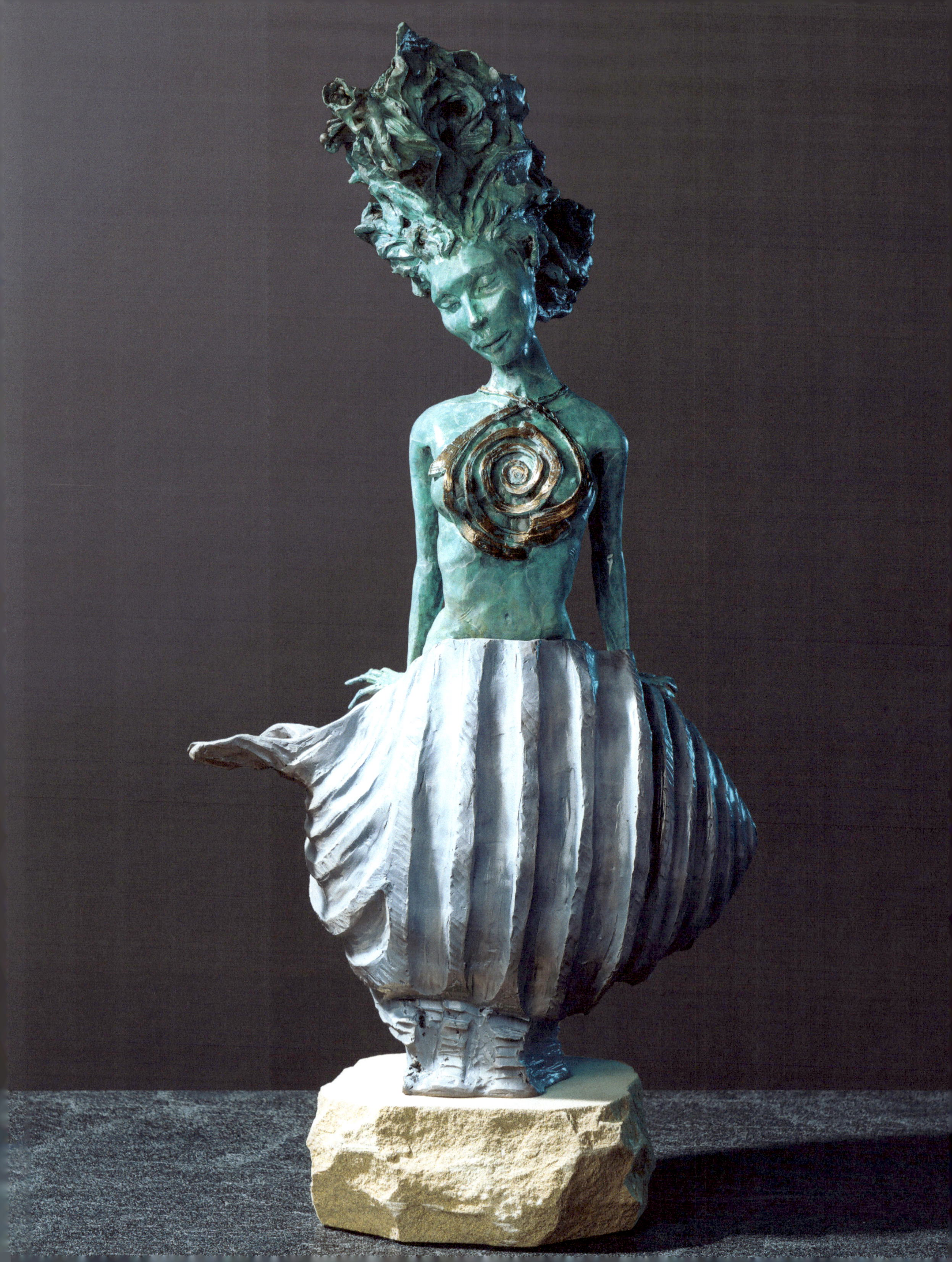

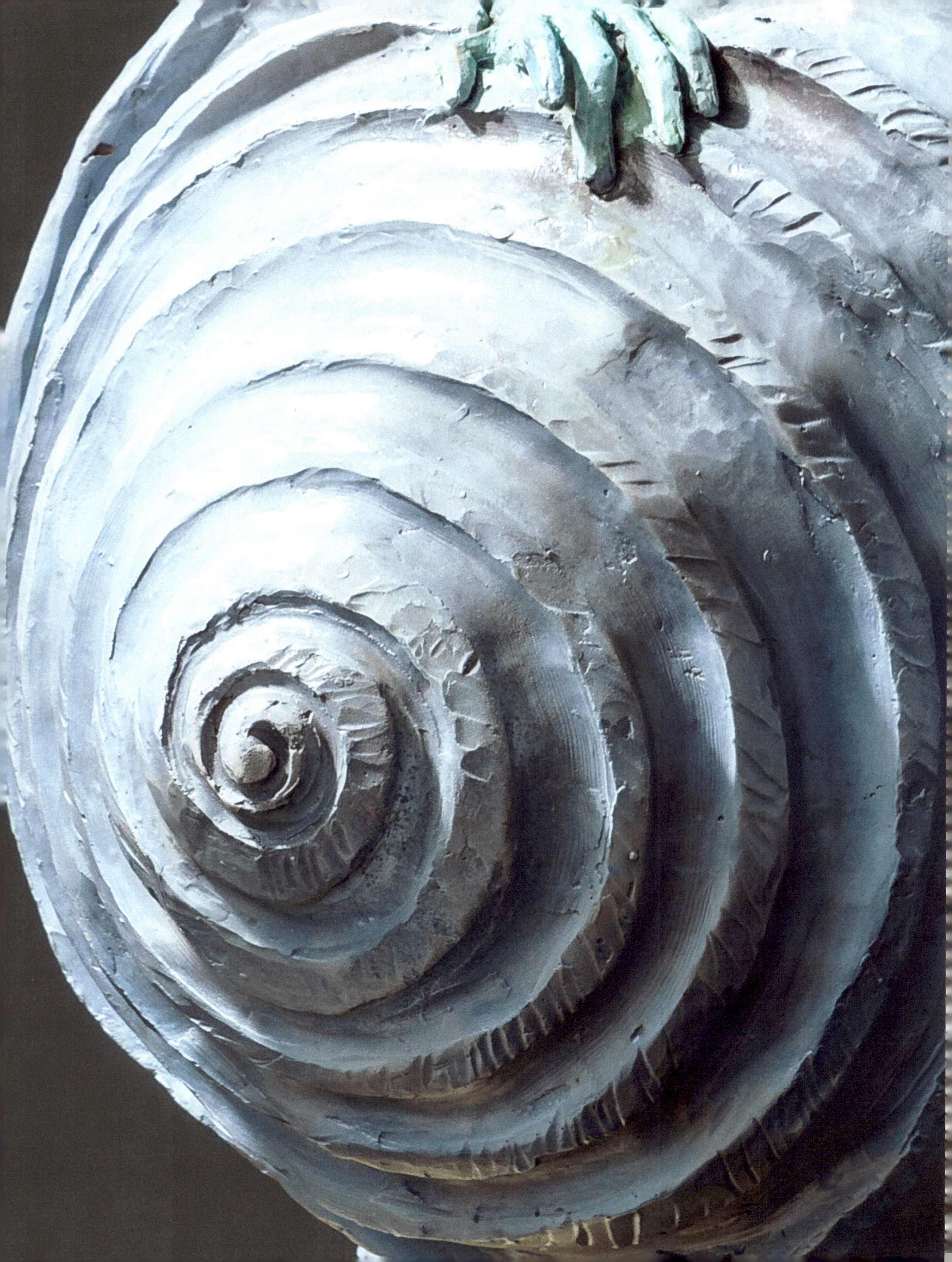

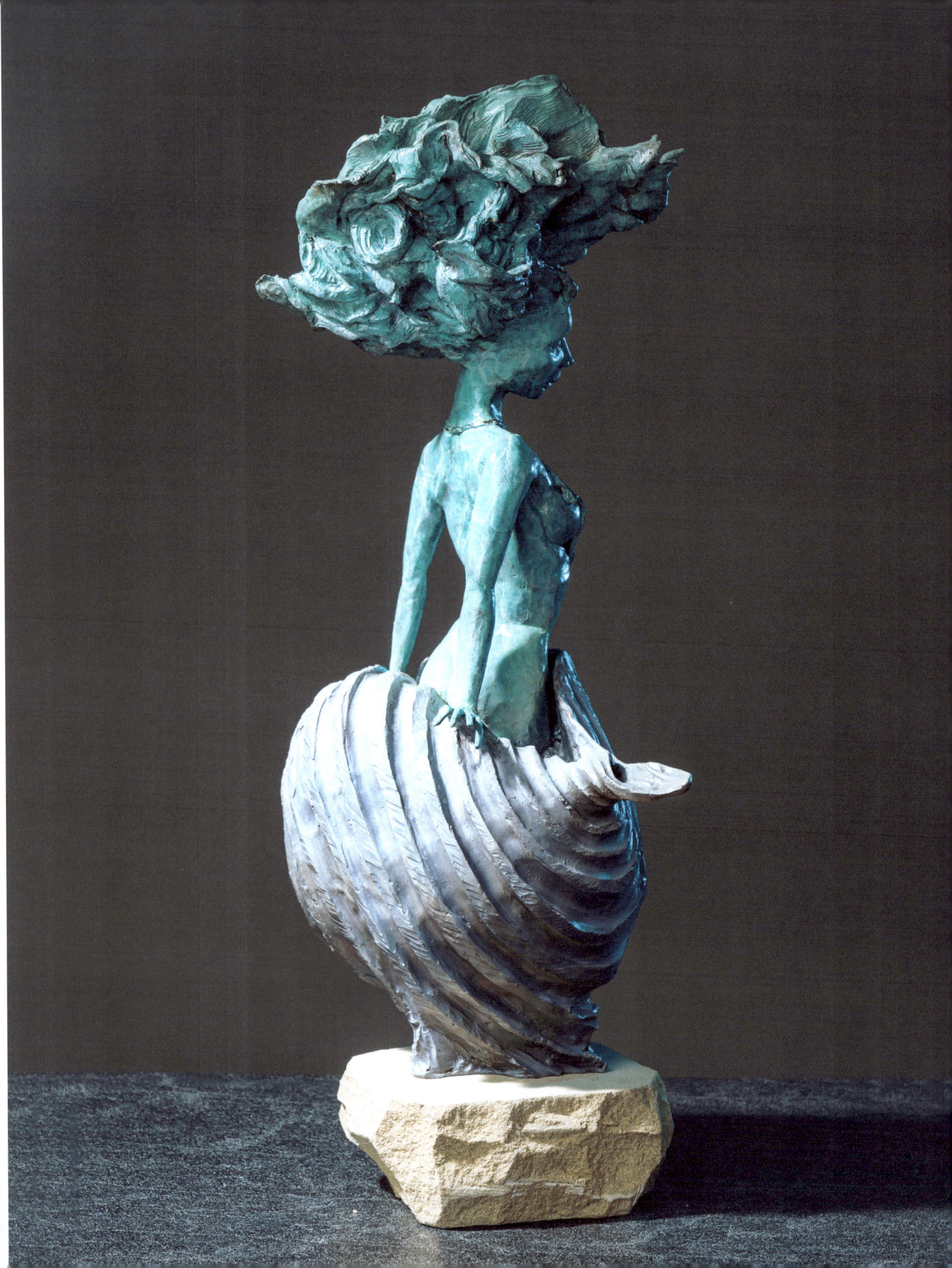

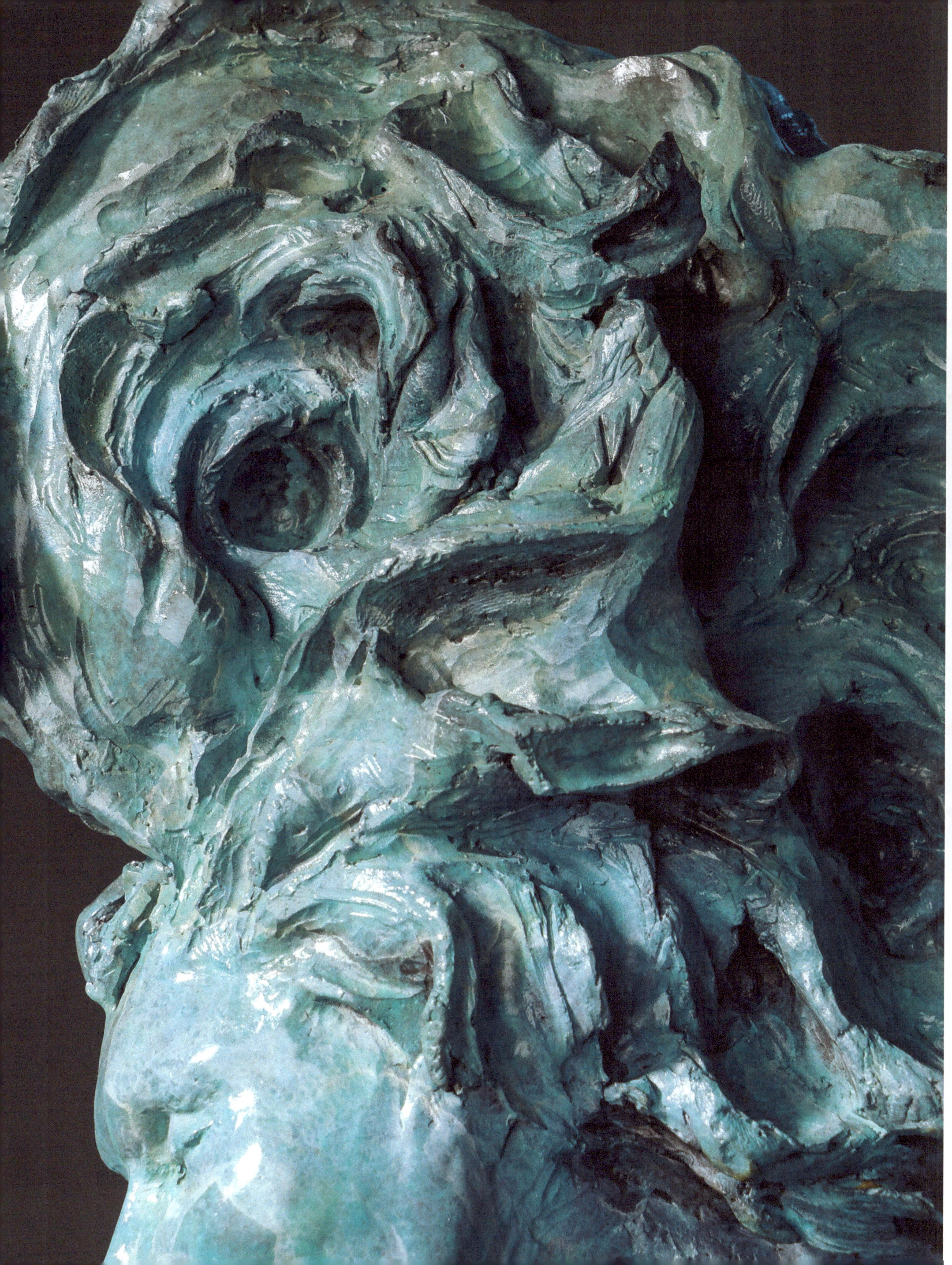

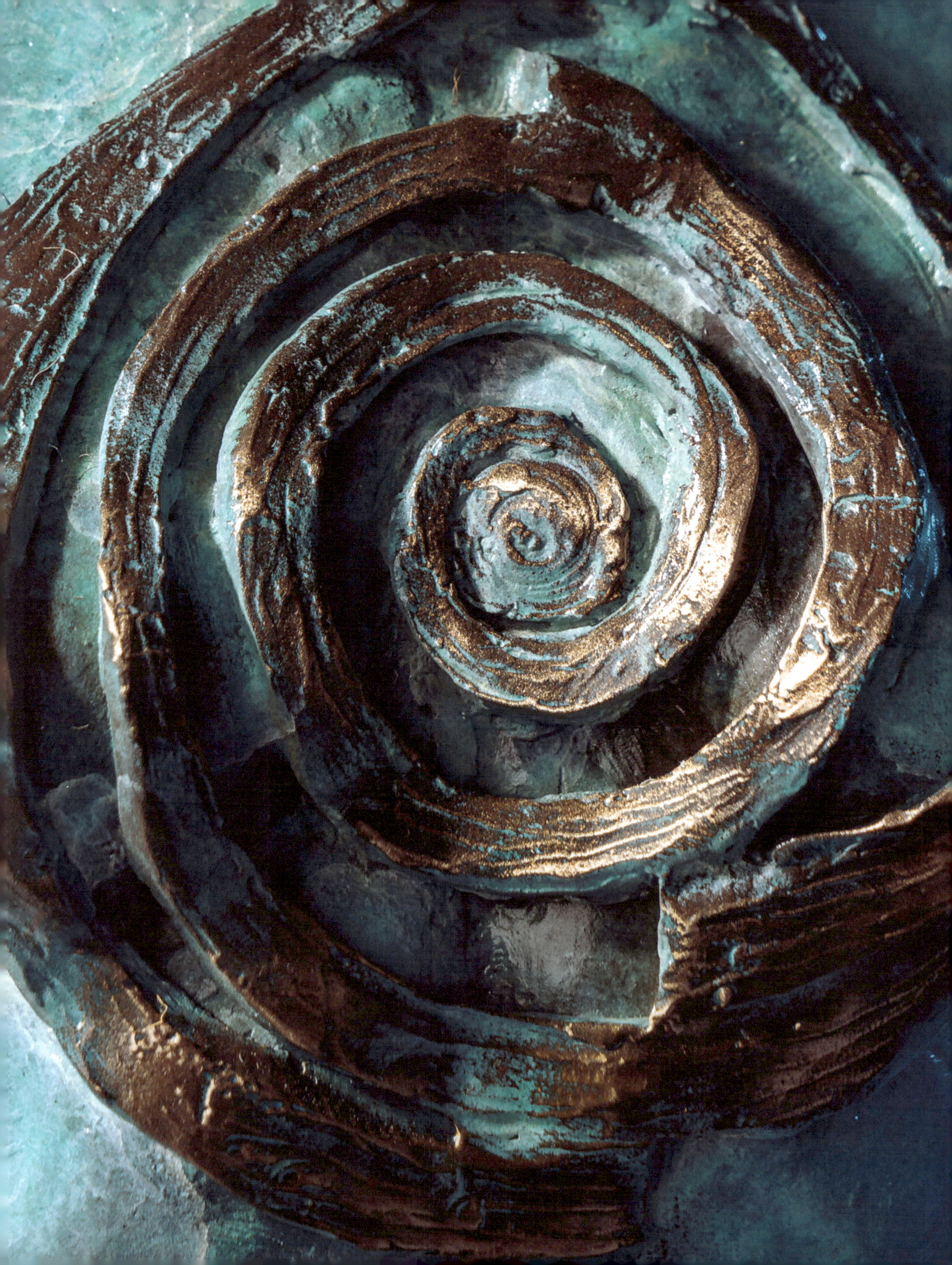

# Ephemeral

This relief had several working titles: Barnacle Girl, Medusa, and a handful of random ones I can't remember.

Ephemeral is one of the five pieces of the Ocean Tides Series, the first relief I ever attemped.

The reason for sculpting this relief was simple: to address why people often don't buy sculptures. "I don't have room," I've heard again and again from people who have plenty of room on their walls for paintings. I love problem-solving, so a relief that hung on a wall seemed the obvious solution.

Ephemeral is a simple sculpture with simple intentions: I wanted to create something that reminded me of a tide pool. I began, not with the ocean, but with this beautiful woman who suggested a depiction I'd once seen of Mother Earth, and then I added barnacles to suggest that she was under water.

The barnacles pushed the sculpture in another direction—and I feared that I'd made a mistake until realizing that I'd stumbled onto something: a theme of personal sacrifice. Suddenly, I saw the woman as a source of life for the barnacles, just as a mother who sacrifices for the growing child in her womb.

The barnacles dotting her skin represent the actions and mental energy she exerts to help others, an honorable legacy impacting myriad lives. I don't tally the good I do, but if goodness is manifested visually on my skin as barnacles, then I'd strive to be completely covered with them.

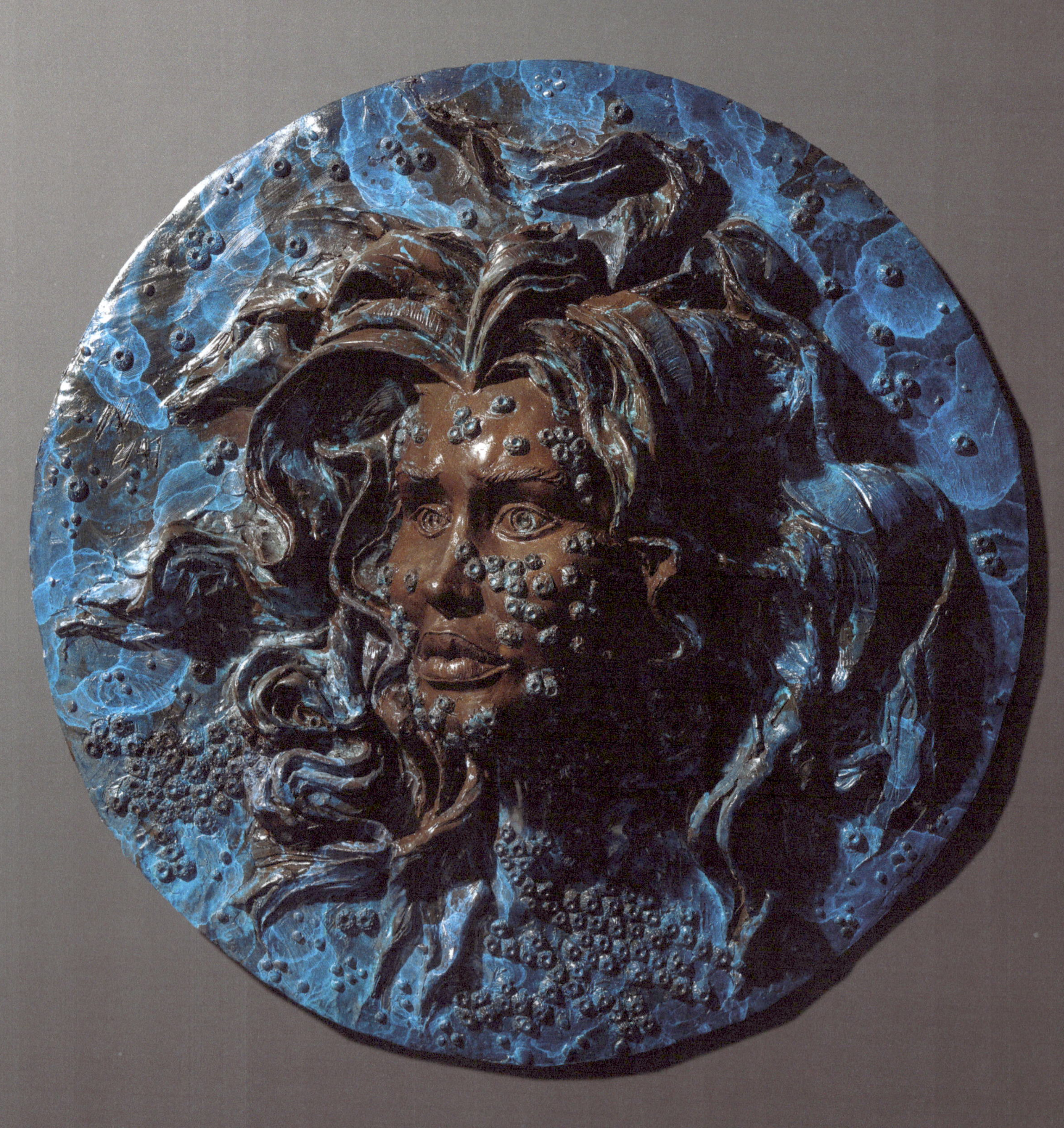

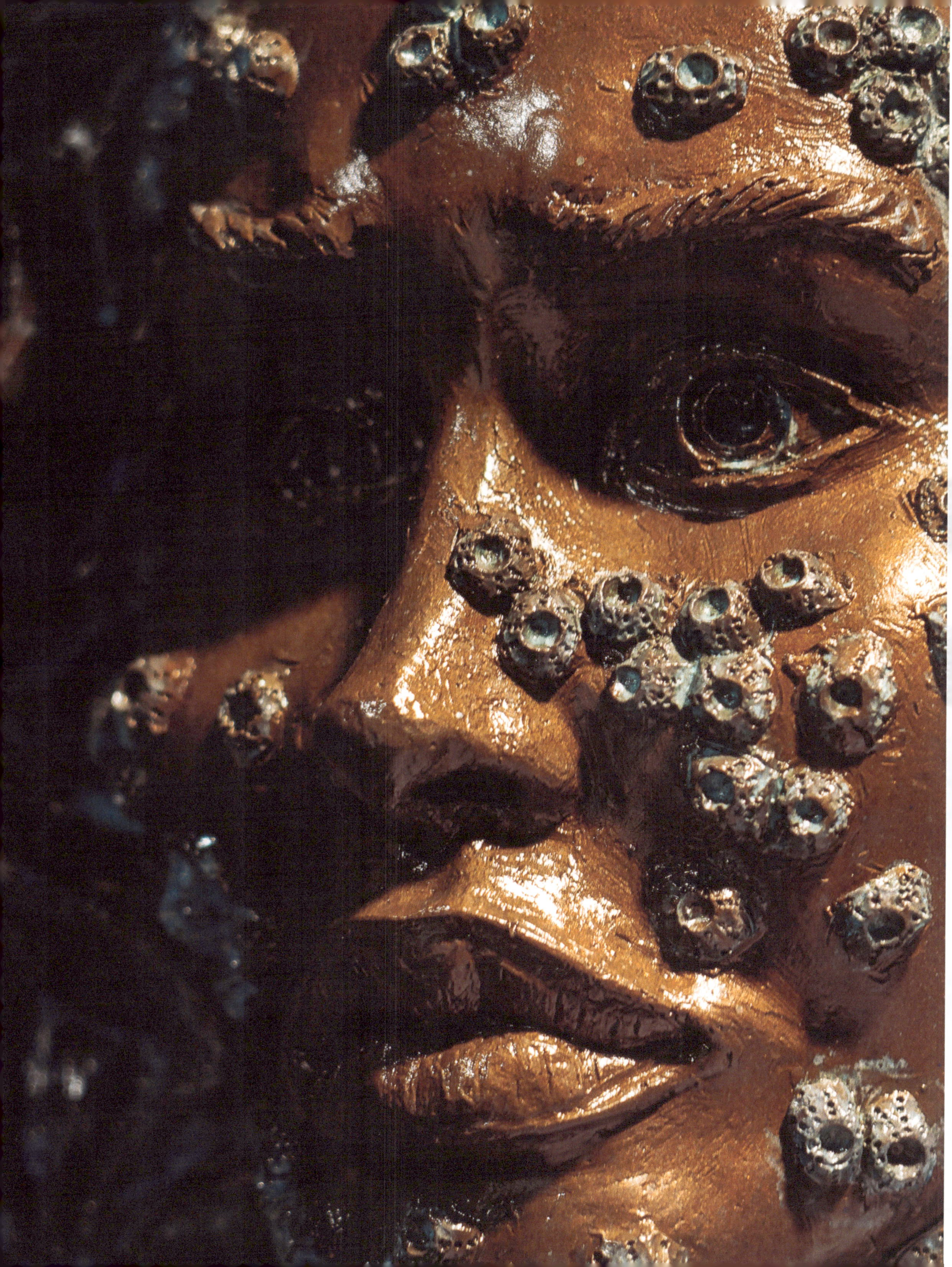

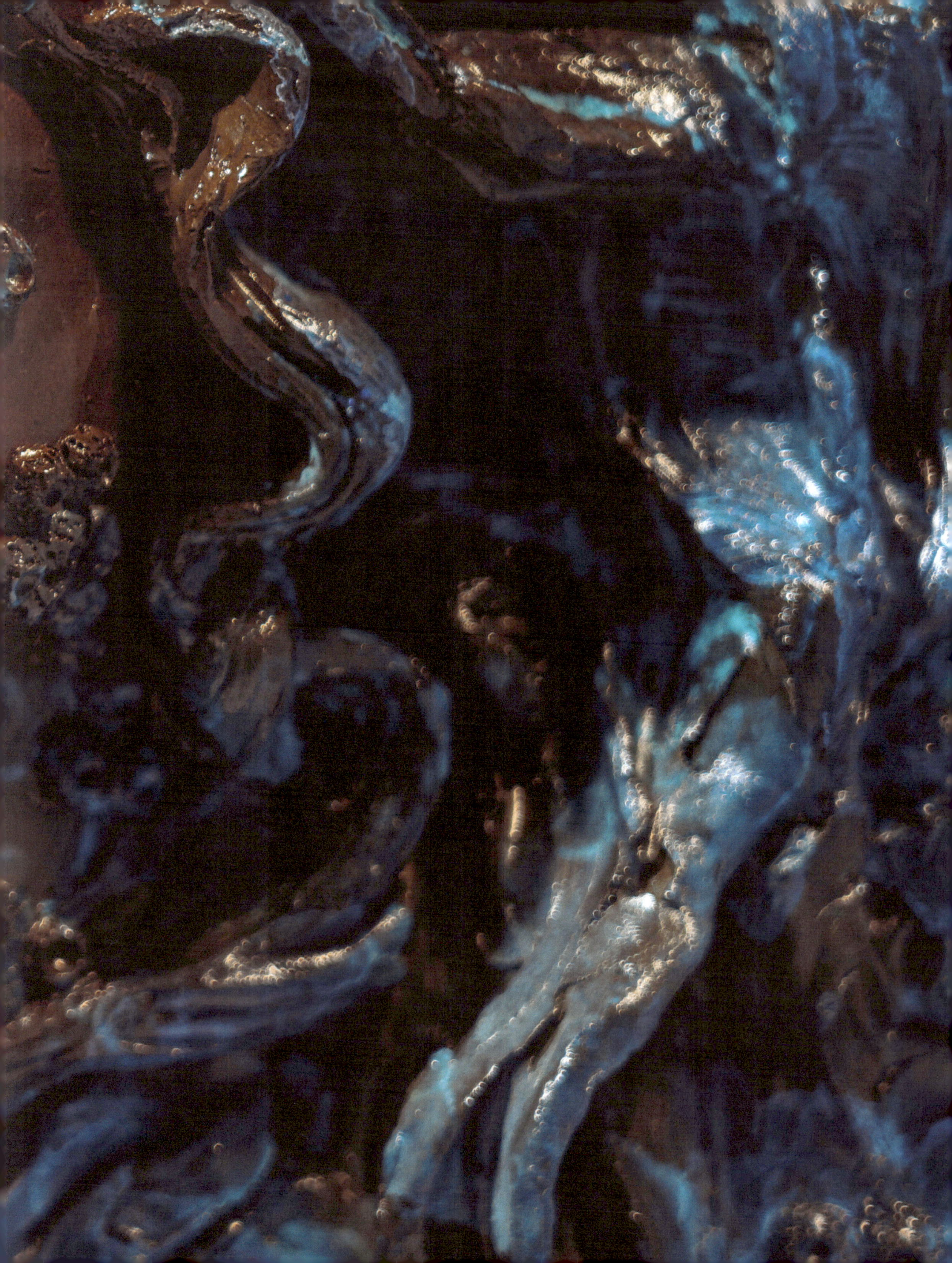

# Sukha

Translated from Chinese, Sukha means happiness, pleasure, ease, joy, or bliss. Through this sculpture, I wanted to infer a sense of lasting happiness.

A Buddhist proverb inspired this piece. The proverb speaks of the road of life, how if we ride in a cart down that road, we interpret the road as bumpy or smooth depending on the quality of the cart's axels. The road is always the same, but the wagon's axles affect our perception of the road.

The power of the mind fascinates me. I believe that the mind, much like clay, takes its form from what influences it. The themes I explore in my sculptures center around our ability to overcome adversity through positivity. Dukka is this piece's contrasting companion: pleasure and pain, happiness and sadness.

As with most sculptures, the challenge is attempting to create a physical representation of an idea so the observer recognizes the meaning behind the form. This piece is no exception to that challenge. Naming it Sukha isn't enough, and for that reason, I hope my words might illuminate a little more of what I'm attempting.

First, there's the form of a warrior, suggesting that happiness, long-lasting and hard-won, requires an ongoing choice to continually battle day after day. Pain and sadness, by contrast, are natural defaults. Those who endure hard things with a positive outlook train their minds to avoid those negative defaults.

Second, there's some nudity, which, for some, has been a point of criticism. I don't take nudity lightly. The form must have a function, so in Sukha, I wanted the nudity to reveal the warrior's youth, naivete, and vulnerability, essential attributes to the story of this sculpture. Some jaded critics might argue that only the young and naïve find happiness. I disagree. Even if we've traveled a long stretch of life on bad axles, we can always repair or replace them.

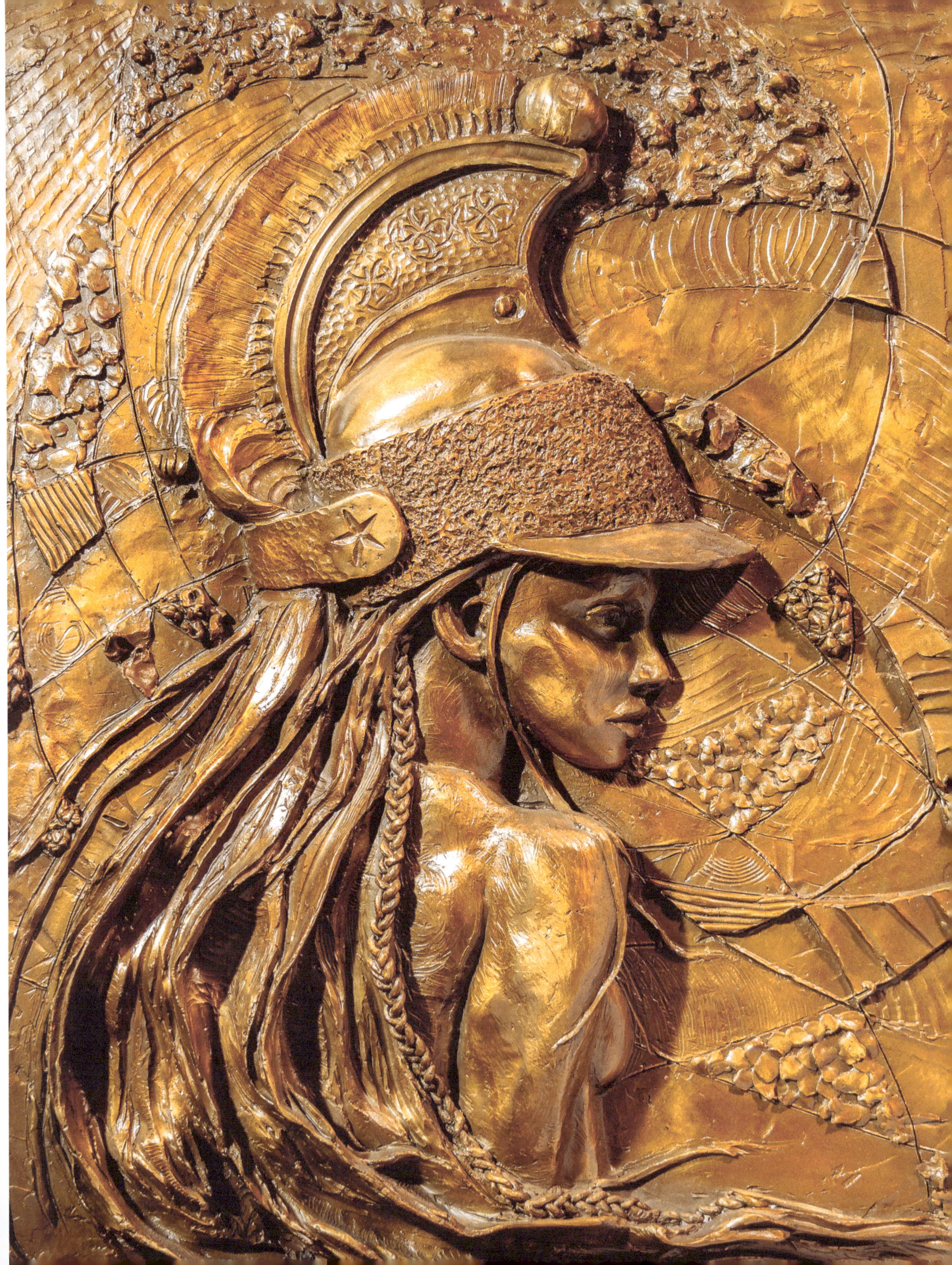

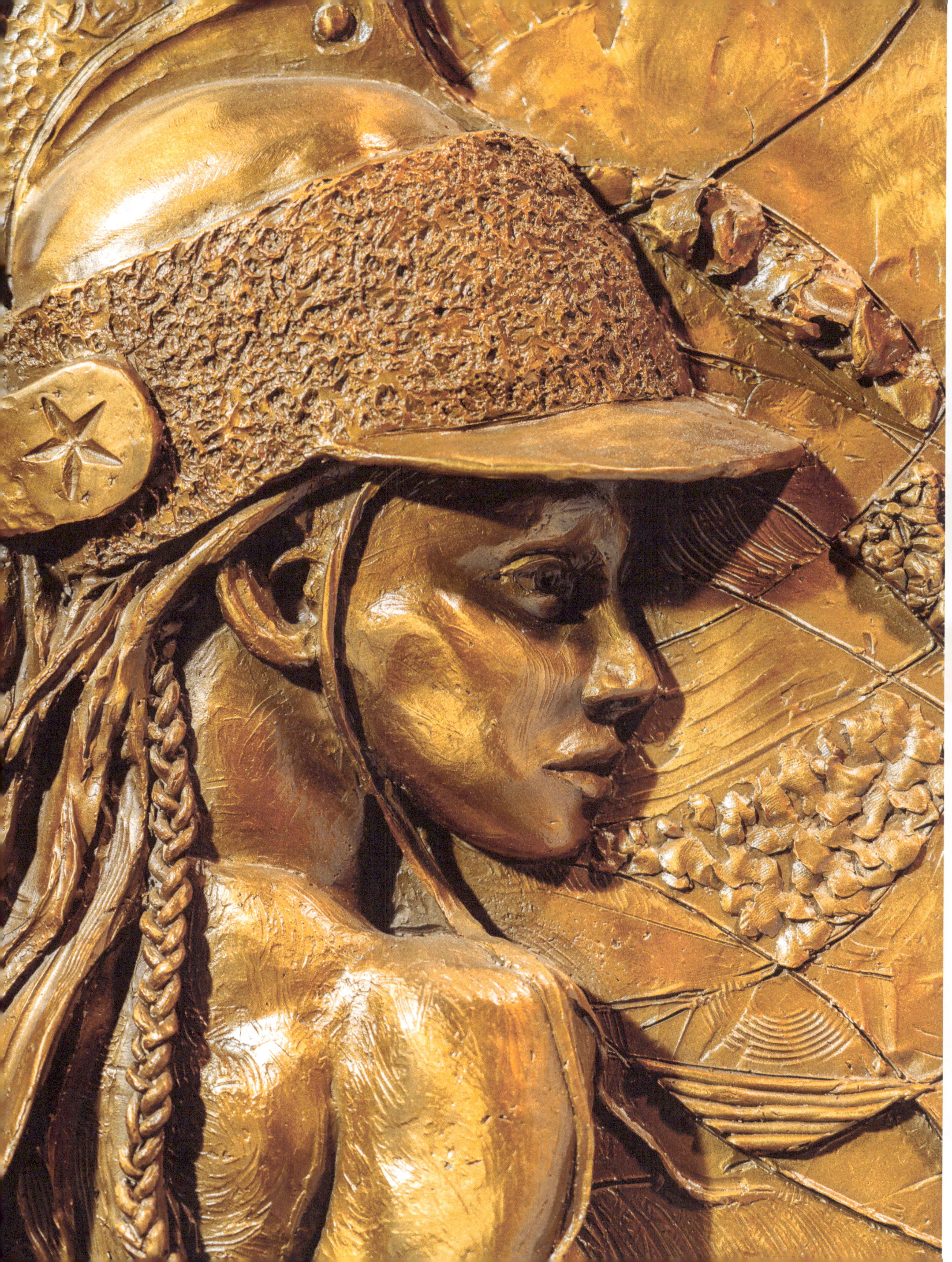

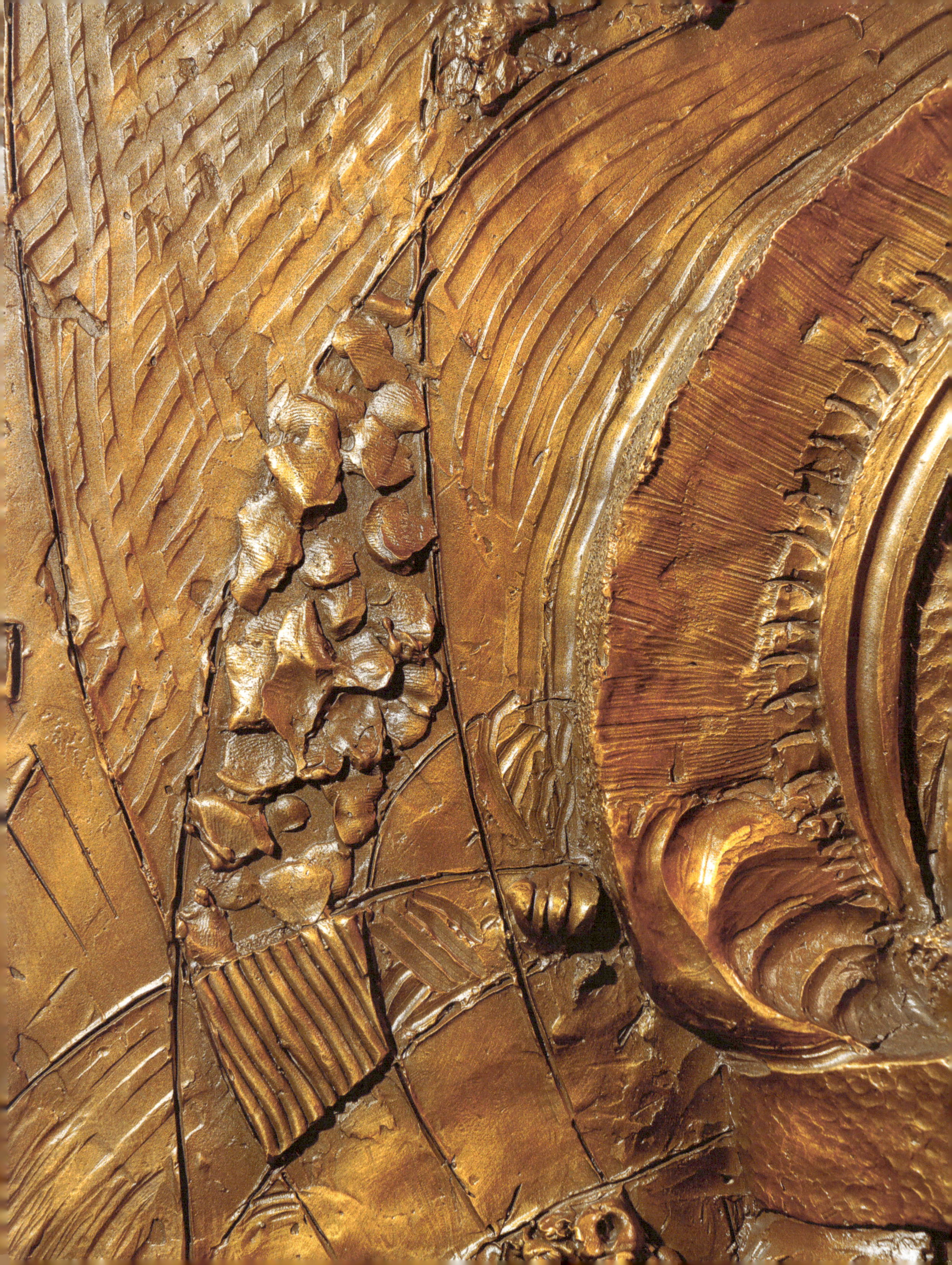

# **Dukkha**

Dukkha is one of the fundamental teachings of Buddhism, and in Pali means pain, suffering, stress, or unhappiness, which connects to three types of suffering: pain, sickness, and death.

When self-preservation is our sole focus, we may misunderstand the role of Dukkha in our pursuit of happiness. For example, in longevity science, one key concept is understanding that death is inevitable and that embracing this alleviates anxiety and fear, thus leading to a longer life.

"Life is meaningless unless you find yourself," Manley Feinberg II asserts in his book Reaching Your Next Summit, a work that challenges us to identify our vulnerabilities and examine our weaknesses while attempting to leverage our strengths. To this, I would add that difficulty and adversity are the fertilizer for growth, and without them, change is slow and maximum potential may never be attained.

Sukah and Dukkah are companion pieces. In Dukkah, again, I portray a warrior whose armor represents the protection we do to avoid pain. When afraid of pain, there is no limit to the amount of armor possibly needed. The warrior carries a staff with a skull, championing death and suffering, a powerful representation to apprise others of her pain. Finally, the background displays of bubbles and flowers provide a contrasting world of stunning colors surrounding this dark figure. With a mindset focused on the bad, even the beautiful can be perceived as negative.

Will we accept life's difficulties? When we experience pain, will we embrace it, knowing that an easy life will never deliver the qualities to truly achieve greatness?

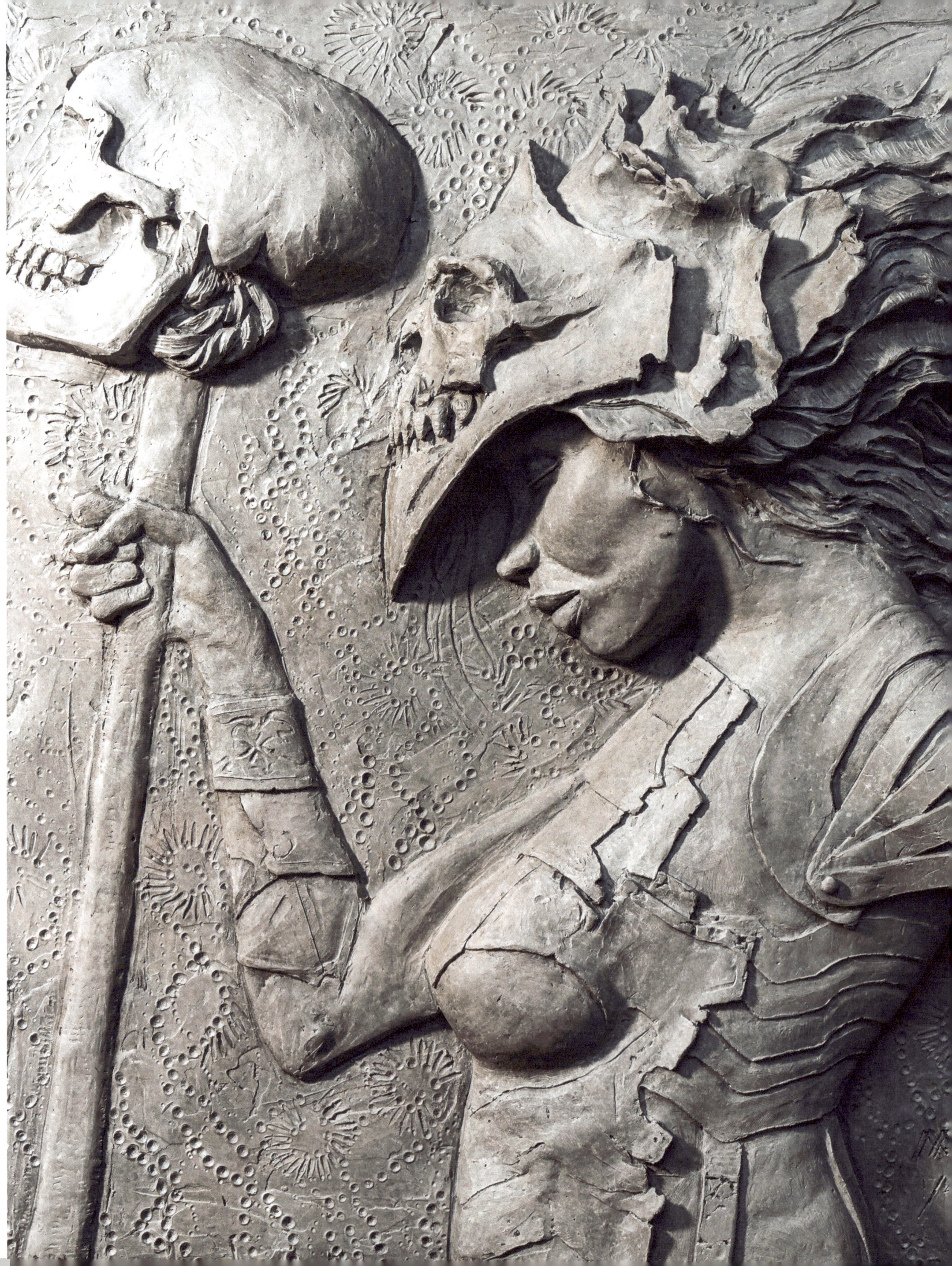

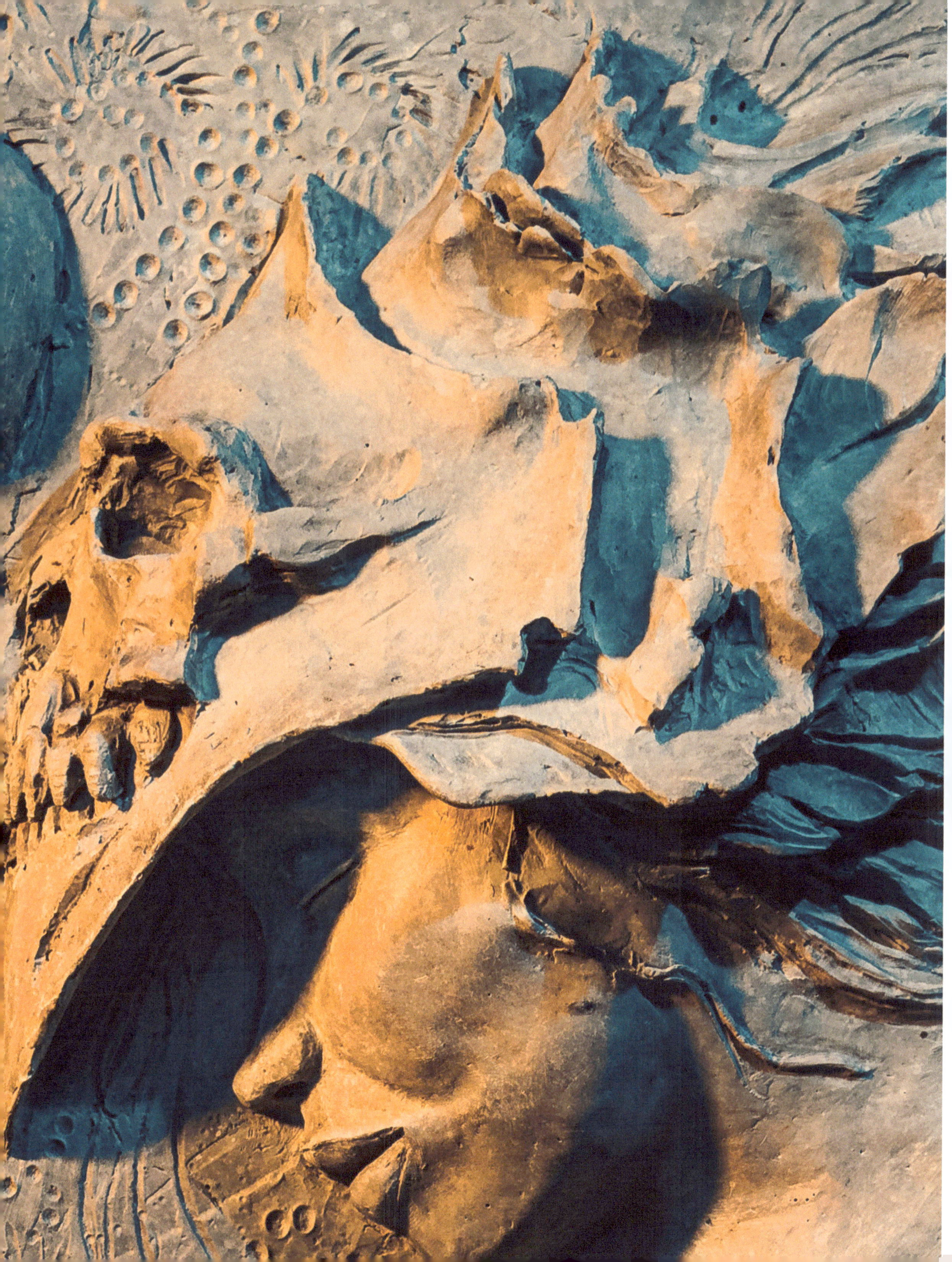

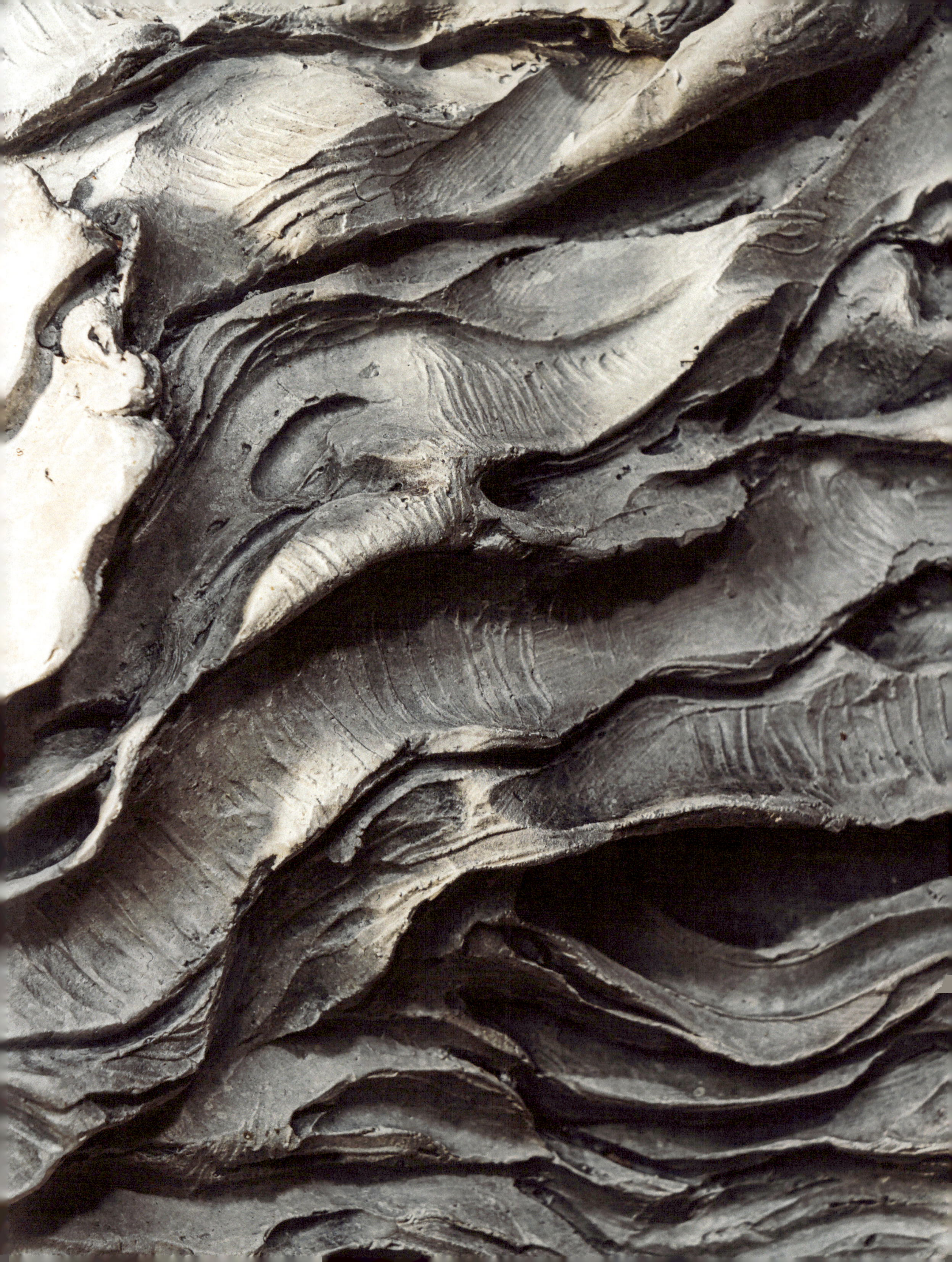

# Blue Man of the Minch

I discovered this mythology when searching for a male counterpart to mermaids. The blue men of the Minch, according to Gaelic mythology, inhabited a stretch of water off the coast of northern Scotland.

The blue men of the Minch appeared human, though their skin was blue, and when the weather was good, they were said to be asleep. When the weather was stormy, they were the cause.

The mythology recounts interactions between sailors and the blue men, how sailors, to avoid tragedy at sea and spare their lives, would finish phrases of poetry started by the blue men.

For me, the blue men of the Minch suggest our need to explore and understand those we don't fully comprehend. While living in Brazil, I heard of an Amazonian person who appeared human in every way, except their feet were turned backward. Those I asked couldn't explain why this was, but they were convinced that these people existed.

Blue Man of the Minch is the perfect counterpart to the dual meaning of Hemeroscopium. There's something deeply mysterious about the ocean that captures our hearts and imaginations. In fact, some of the elements of the sculpture reflect what my family and I have seen in tide pools, the different forms of life in various shapes and colors.

I feel Blue Man of the Minch prompts me toward self-exploration through a series of questions: What are the stories I tell myself? Have I created myths to explain what I don't understand? Do I see things as they truly are? Or have I formed ideas based on the stilted opinions of others? If so, the antidote to closed-mindedness is open-mindedness and valuing the opinions of others.

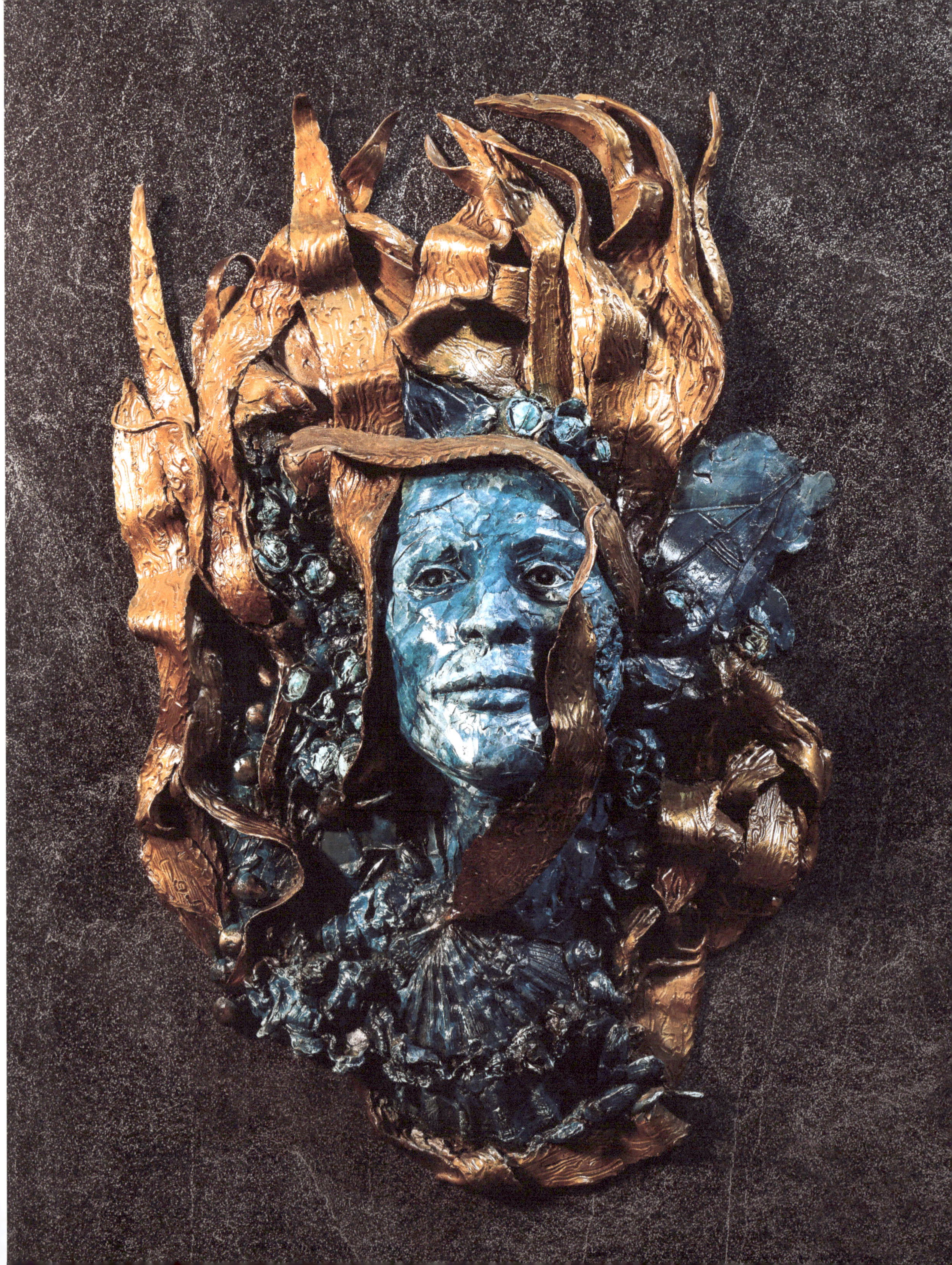

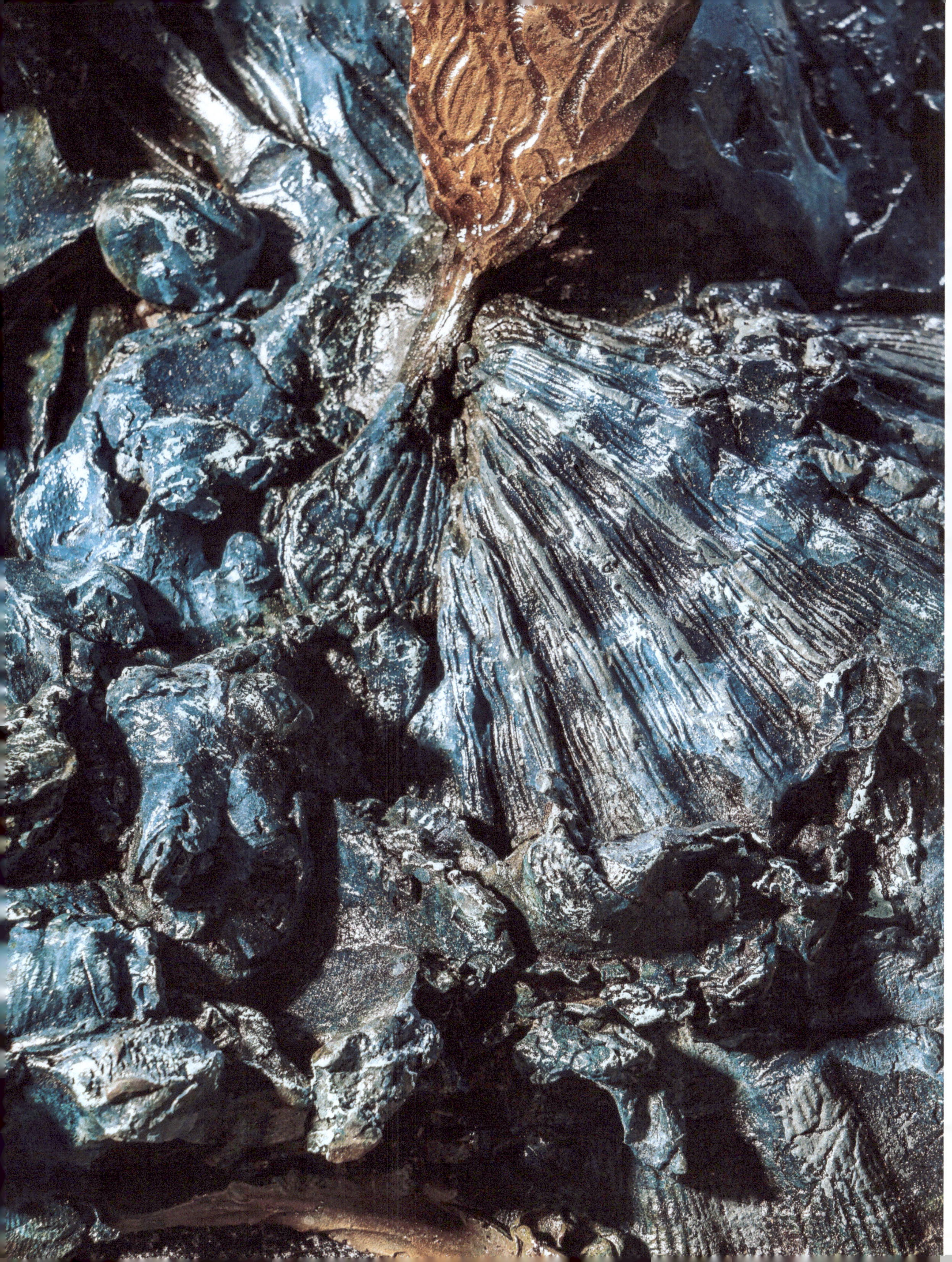

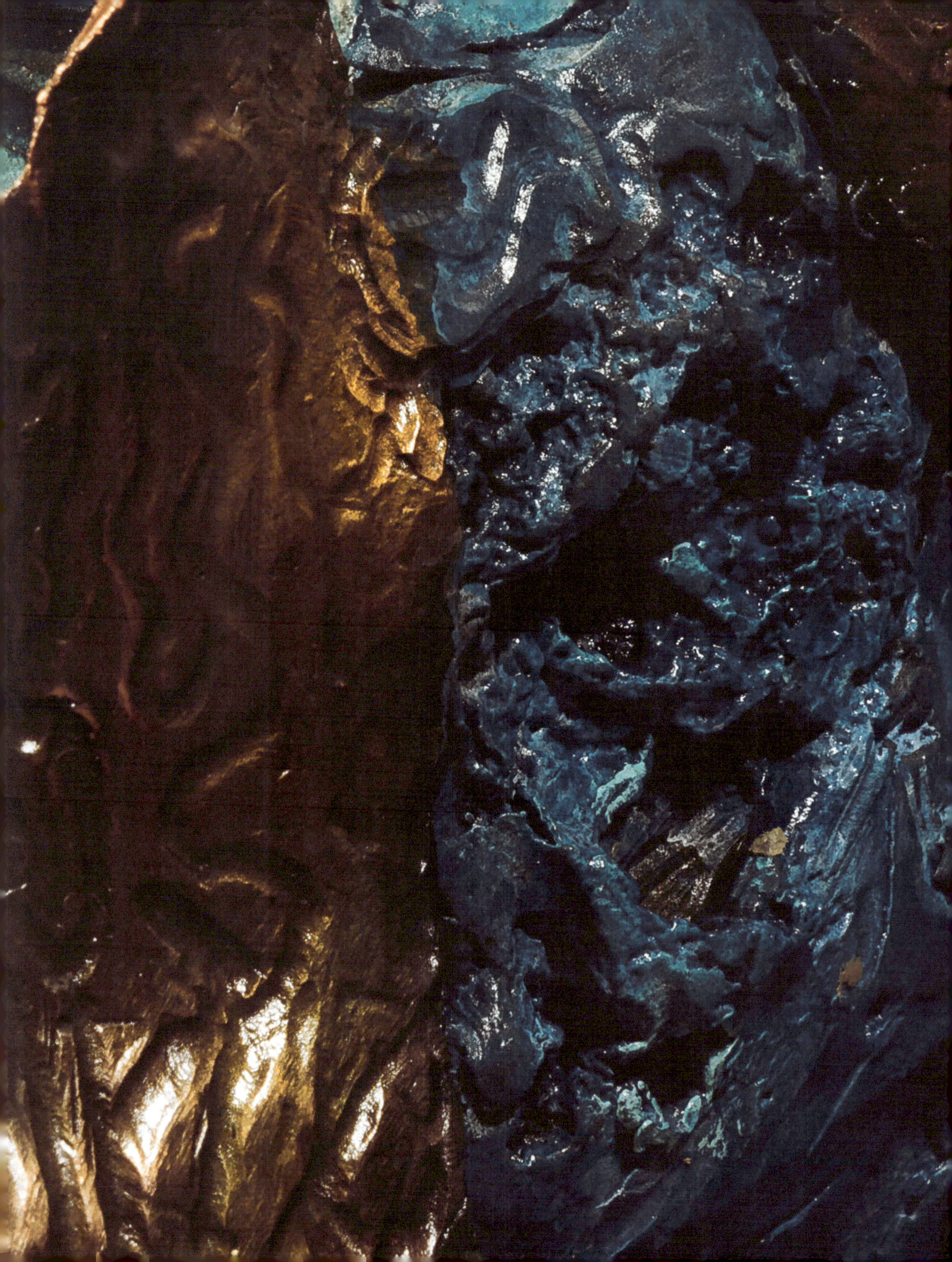

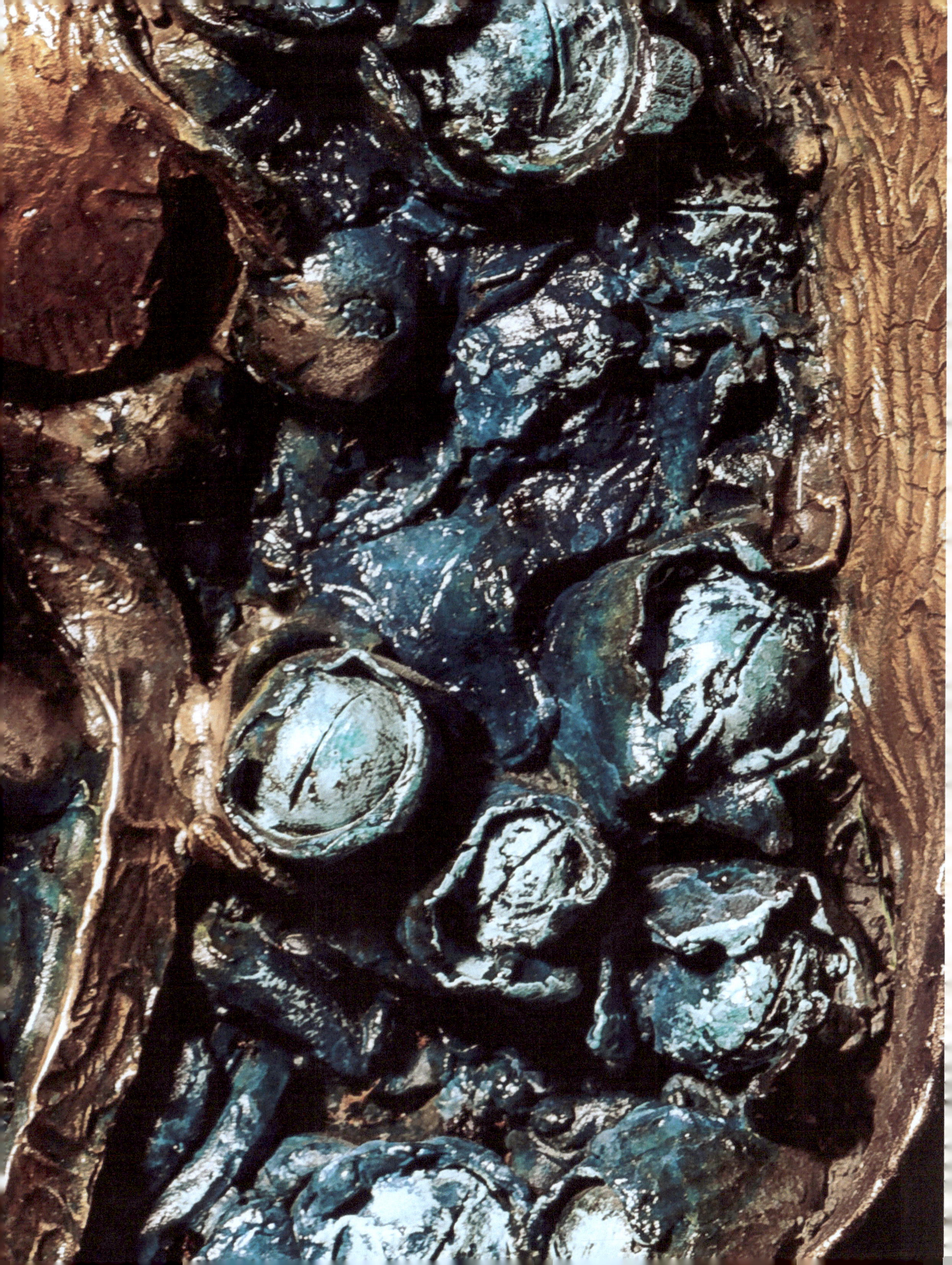

## Freed by Forgiveness

Sometimes our knowledge is too indirect, and so to achieve true understanding, we require firsthand knowledge.

The great lessons of life may require pain and suffering and, with them, a knowledge that embeds in our character. Freed by Forgiveness explores this concept.

The idea began to take root just after I finished reading a book that explored the profound power of forgiveness. After absorbing each amazing story in that book, I felt compelled to sculpt something to communicate those ideas.

Partway through this project, I witnessed a robbery. At first, I was confused about what was happening. Those also witnessing the robbery encouraged me not to get involved, worried for my safety, which I appreciated. Yet, I felt ignoring the robbery was morally wrong. After all, if we aren't willing to protect our beliefs, perhaps we don't deserve our freedoms. Because of my hesitancy and the hesitancy of those around me, the thieves escaped.

Once before, I'd witnessed a robbery like this one, and that experience taught me to be alert and decisive—but that was a long time ago. Enough time had passed, and I was unprepared. Somebody could have been harmed. That thought looped endlessly through my mind. In fact, for days after the robbery, my mind, when idle, returned to the crime. I couldn't sleep. I was angry at the thieves, at the store employees, at the bystanders—and angry at myself. Trapped and ensnared through no fault of my own, I didn't know how to rid myself of this anger. How could I find peace?

And then an epiphany! I could only be responsible for my own actions. For me to heal, I had to forgive myself.

At that moment, a burden was lifted, replaced with an immediate relief. For the first time in weeks, I could draw in a deep breath. That epiphany healed my soul.

The man in this sculpture is blindfolded to show his myopia and naivete to what can potentially harm us. Offenses, grudges, revenge, and hatred—nets and chains like hidden dangers that sink our souls. Forgiveness is the only true path to complete freedom. Forgiveness frees.

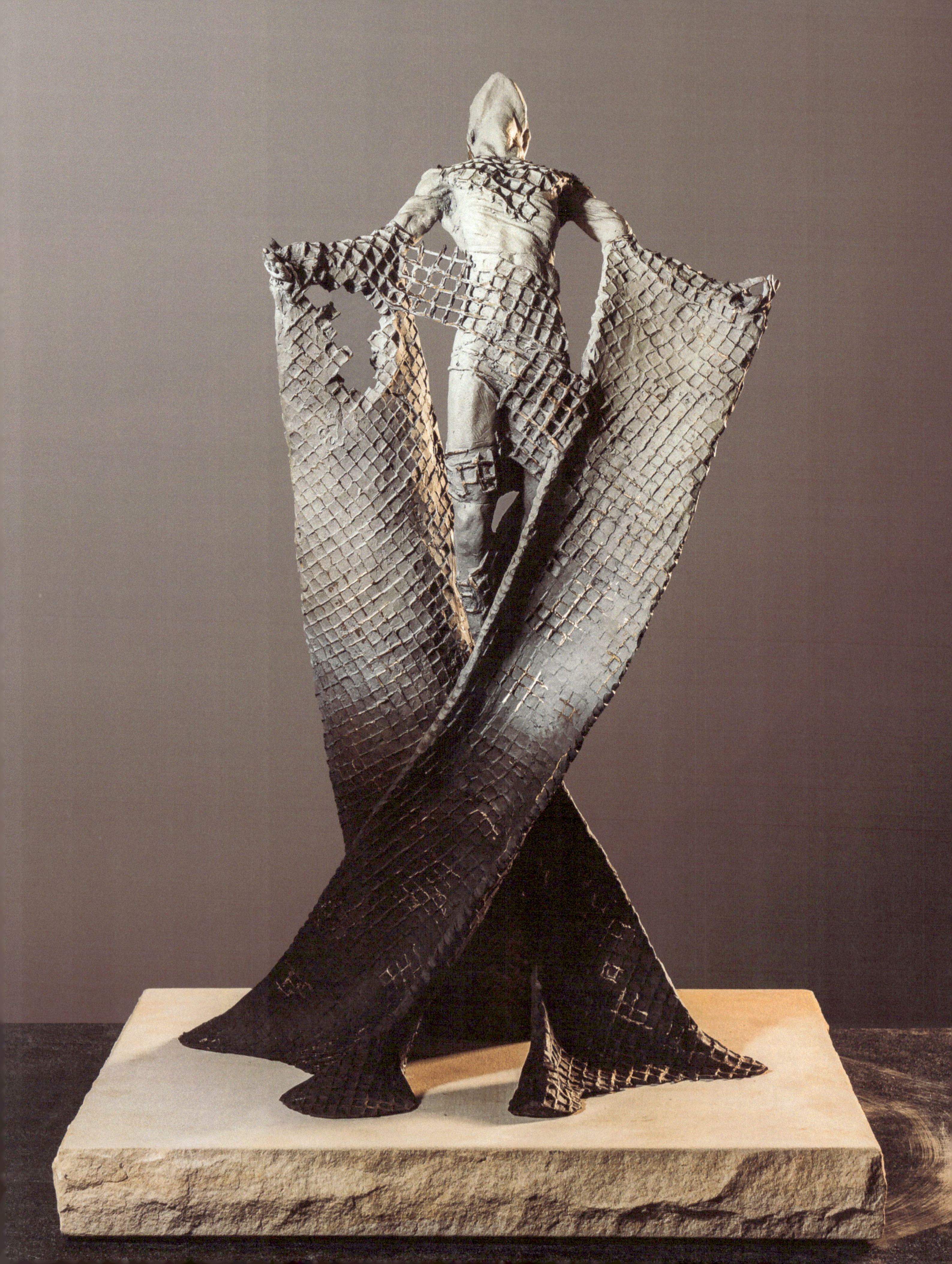

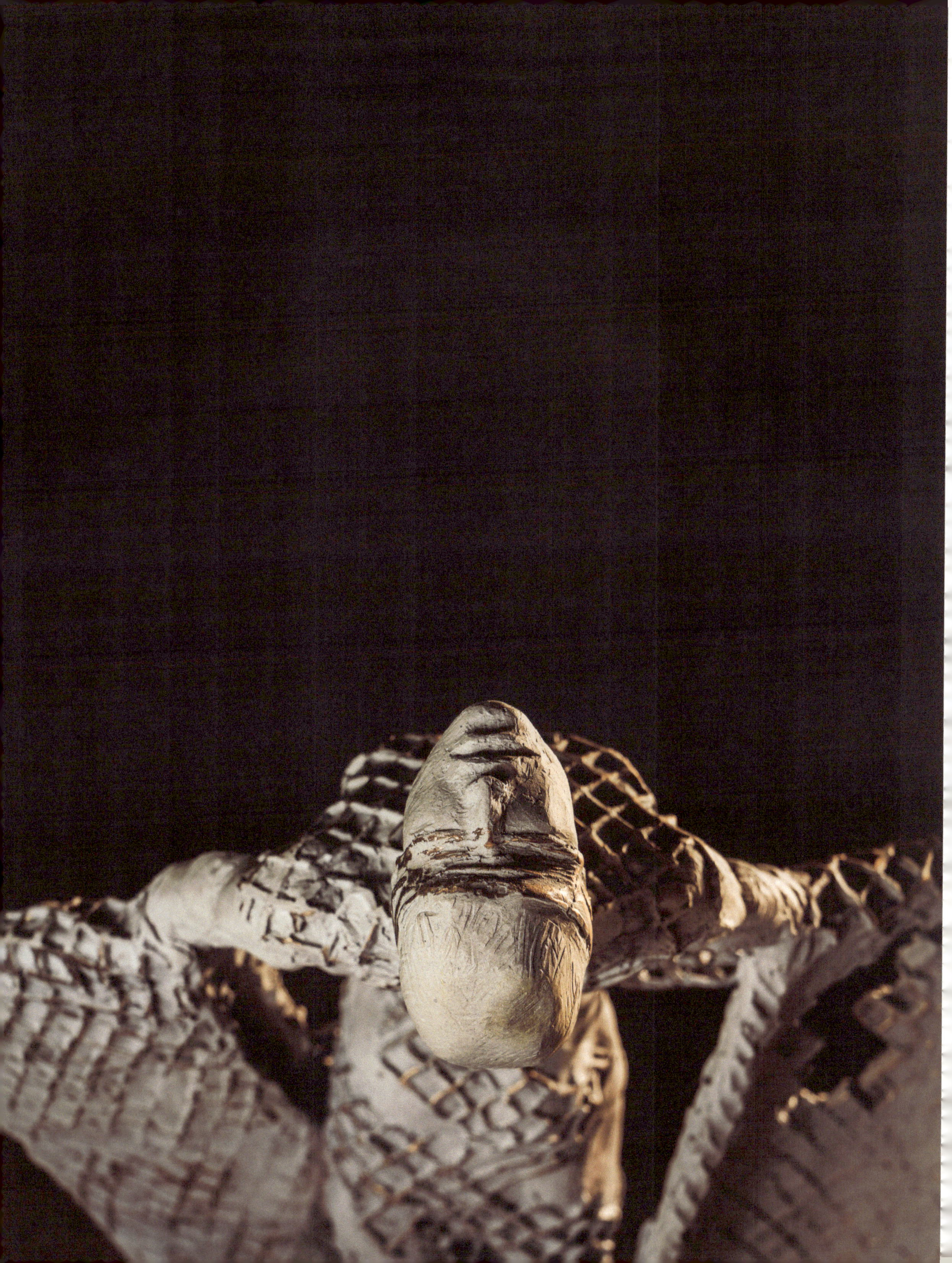

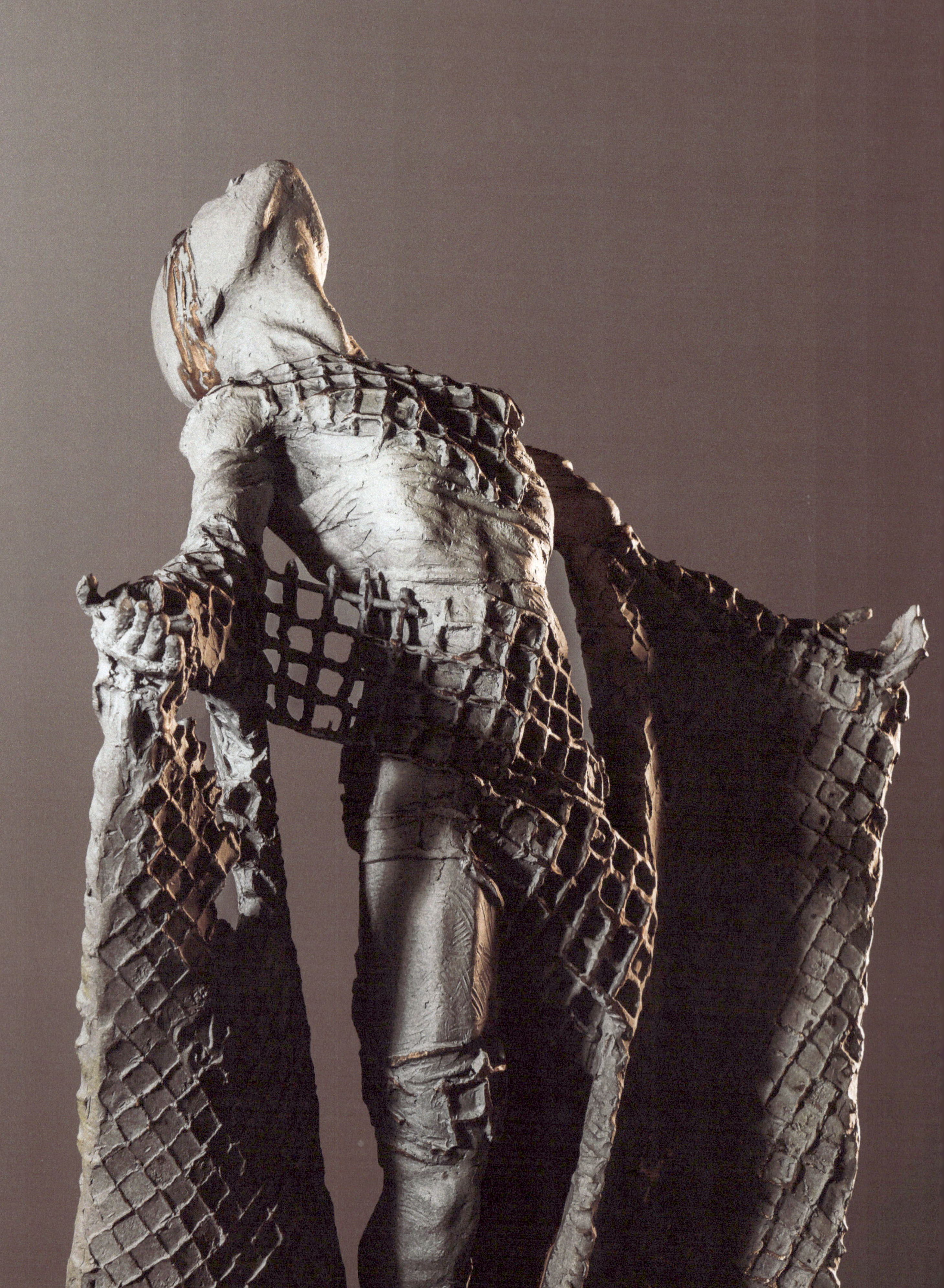

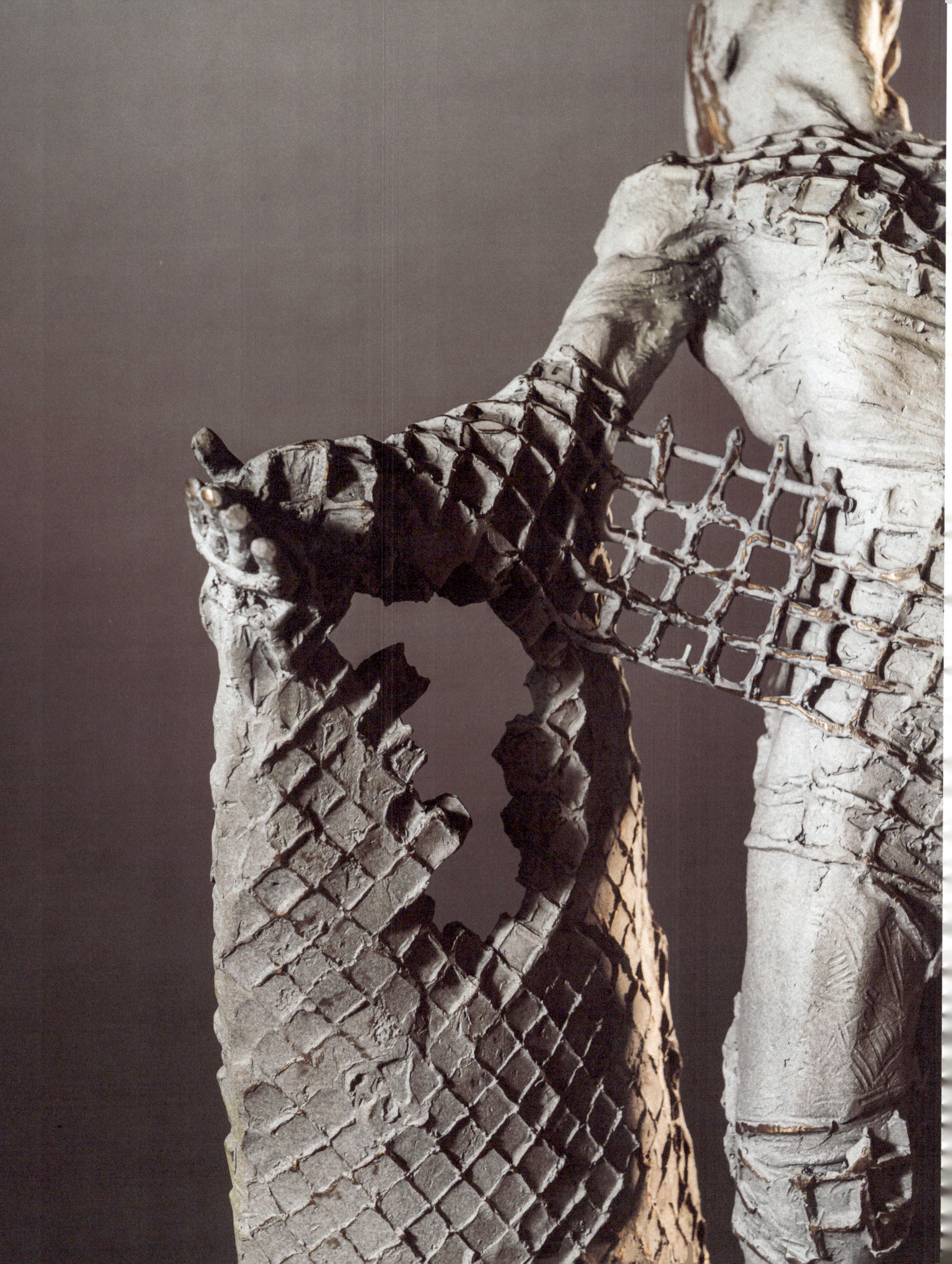

# Perception

I wanted to explore how we see ourselves versus reality, to show the wisdom that emerges with experience as our self-image changes depending on which side of the mirror we view ourselves. Our eyes can lie to us.

Perception explores two sides of the mirror, one where a younger woman identifies her every possible flaw, while her older self, with the wisdom of time and experience, smiles with adoration and appreciation at what she sees: a younger, more beautiful version of herself.

This is one of my favorite sculptures because of the way so many people relate to it, connecting to it and discovering applications in ways I'd never considered. One challenge of this piece was creating the effect that this was the same person. When observers see this sculpture from one end, I love how they think there's a mirror. It fools everyone until they view the two figures straight on and see the illusion. Again: our eyes can lie to us.

Another aspect of the deception is in the two figures. I toyed with creating them almost identical, yet that's a problem when attempting to show folds falling off different proportions. For example, if one woman is slightly shorter from the aging process, her clothing will fit differently. Conversely, clothing presents in another way on a slightly larger form, a difference I wanted to show.

Further, I wanted to show how nothing escapes our critical eye when we judge ourselves, thus the sheer clothing that hides nothing.

Lastly, I chose to explore how our analysis, experiences, and biases color our observations by replicating a larger, similar mirror that frames the entire piece and includes whoever views it. I want observers of this piece to consider if they are immune to that human tendency of self-judgment. I want them to ponder which side of the mirror they are on.

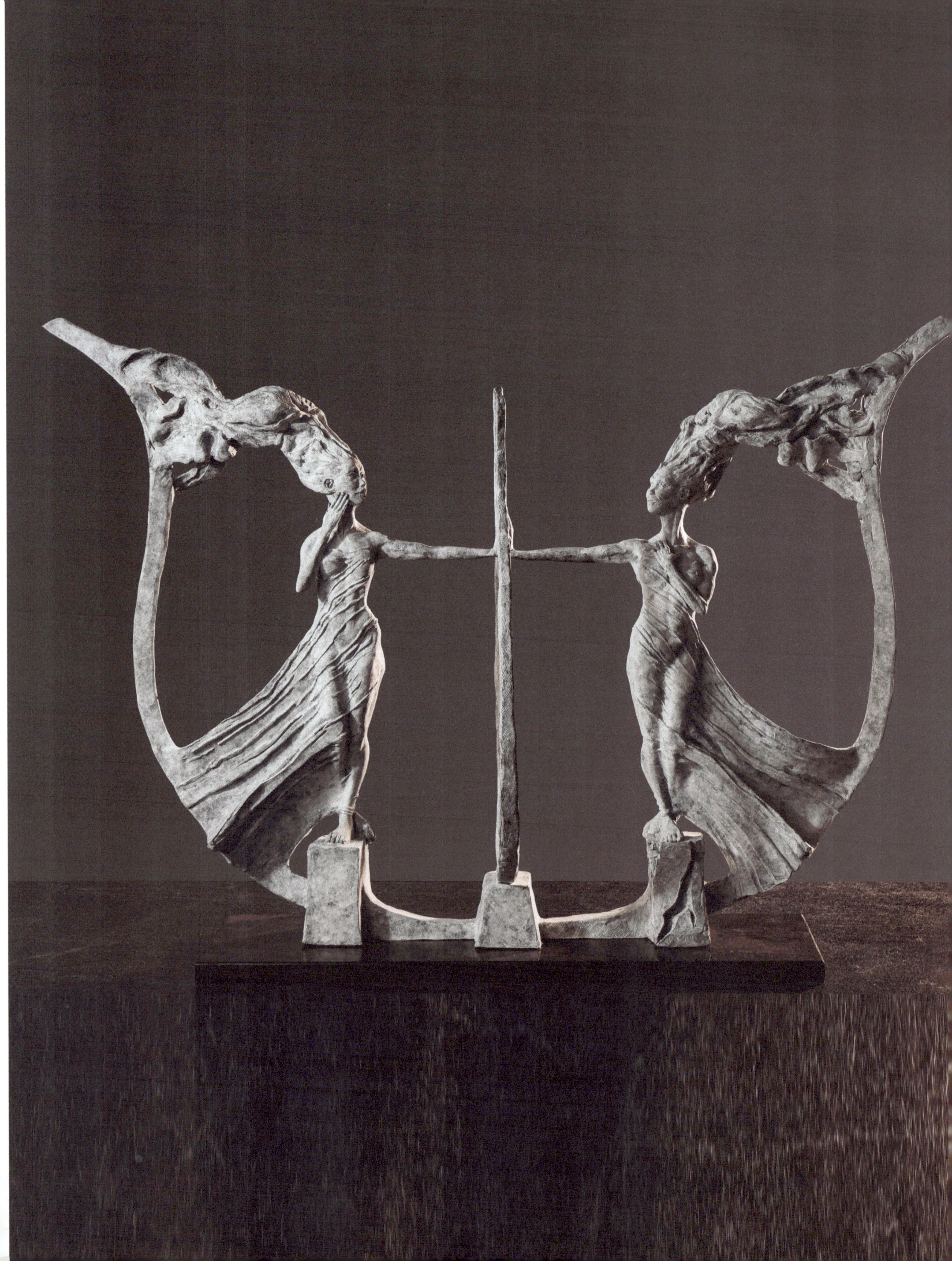

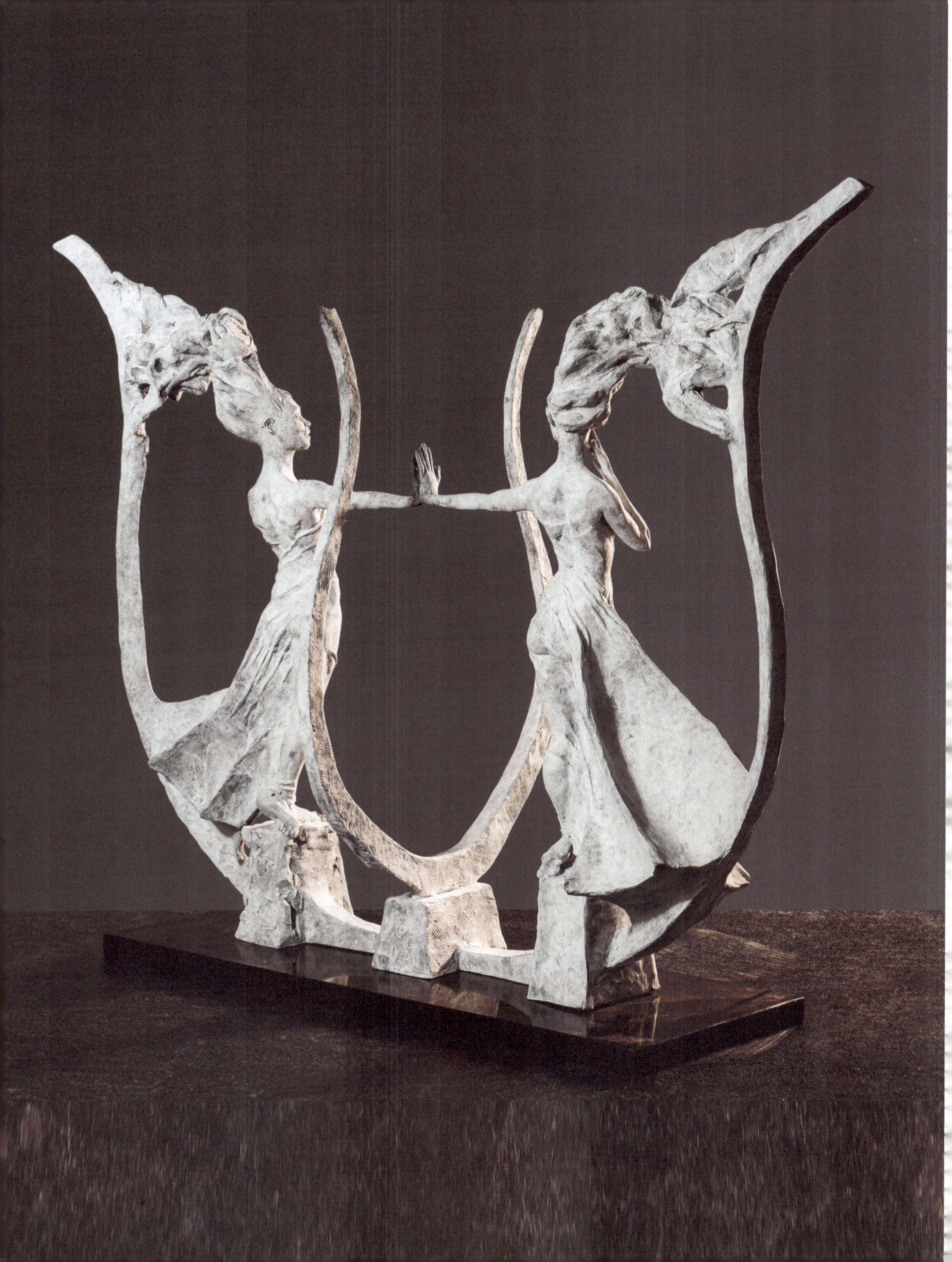

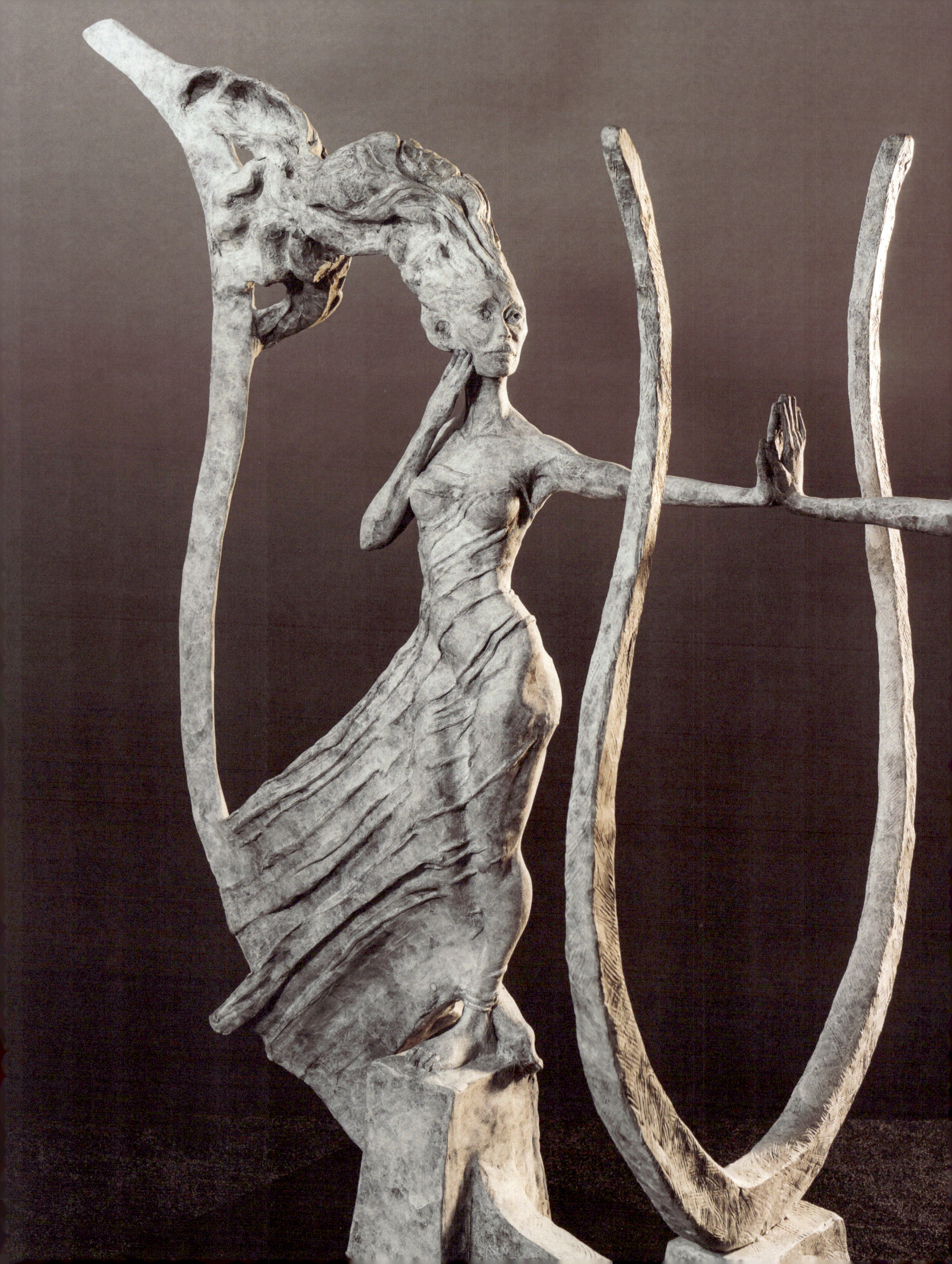

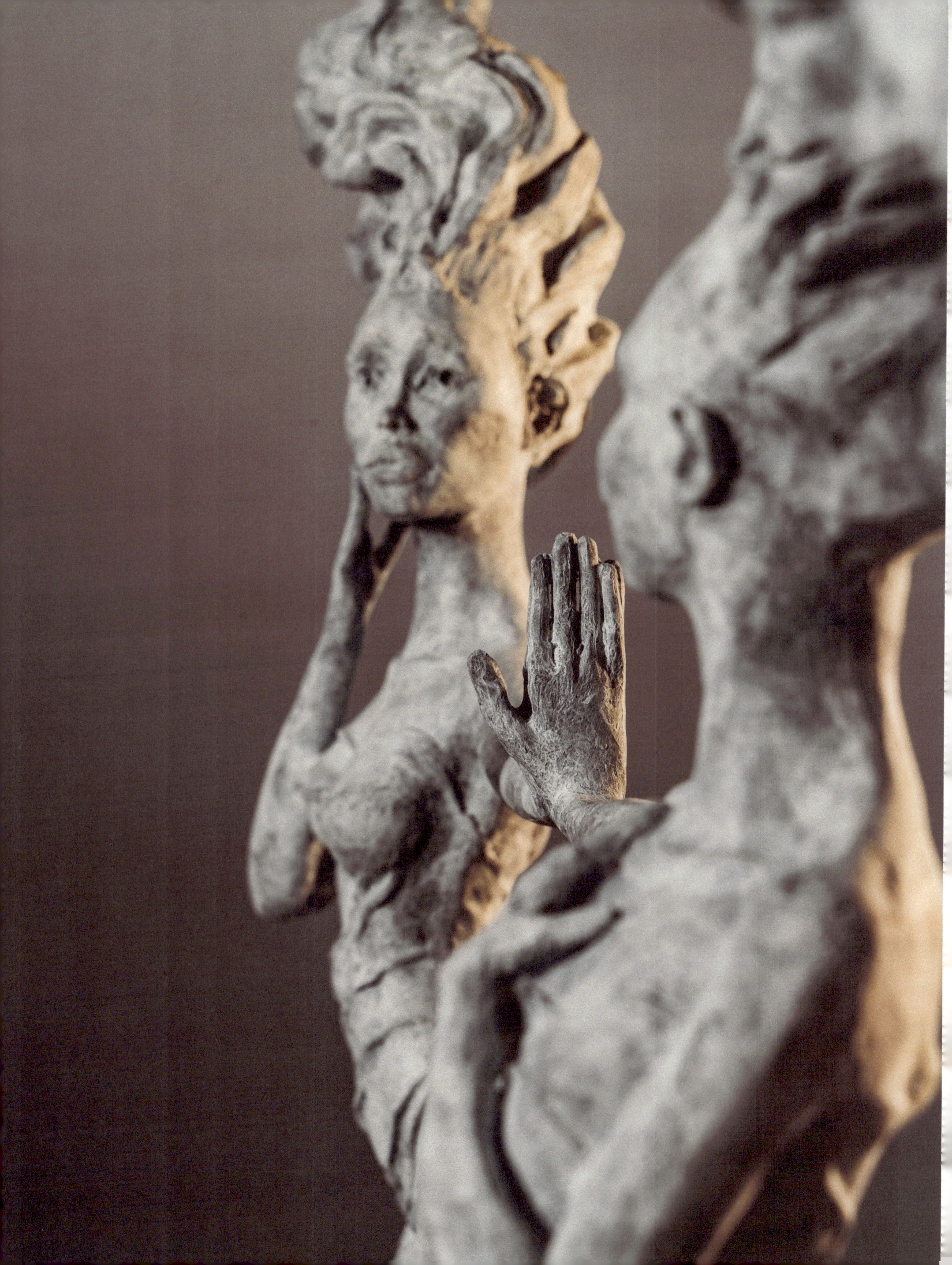

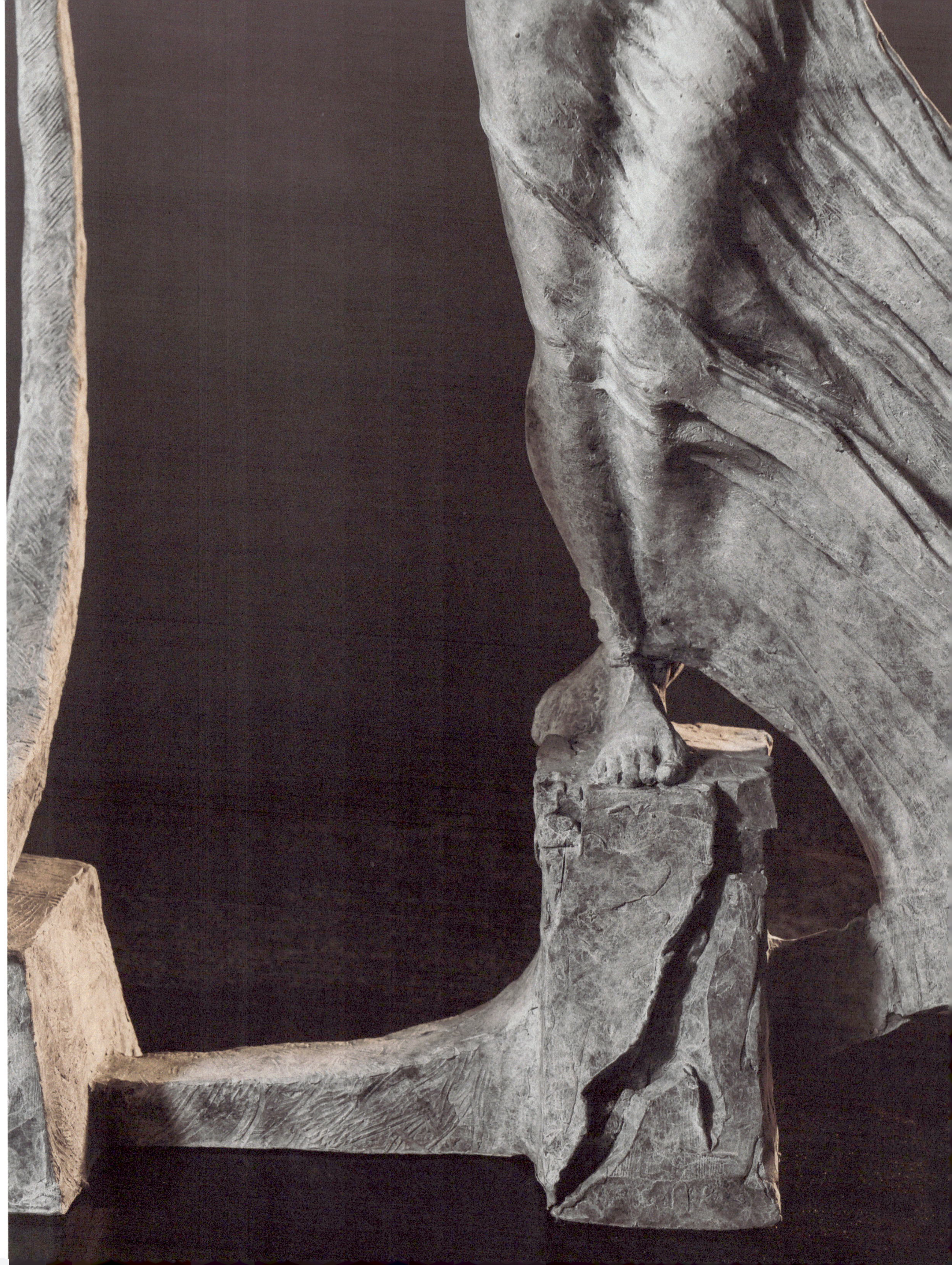

# List of Illustrated Works

*Dimensions given are height by width by Depth*

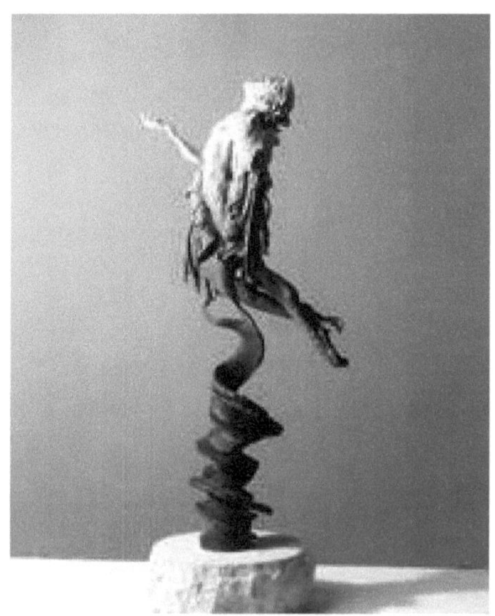

*Page 11- 18*
*After the Fall, 2023*
*Bronze*
*28 x 10 x 10 inches*

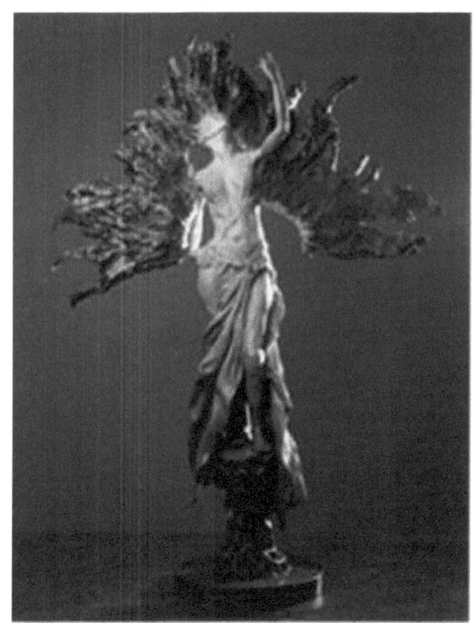

*Page 19 - 27*
*Sunrise, 2021*
*Bronze*
*35 x 13 x 9 inches*

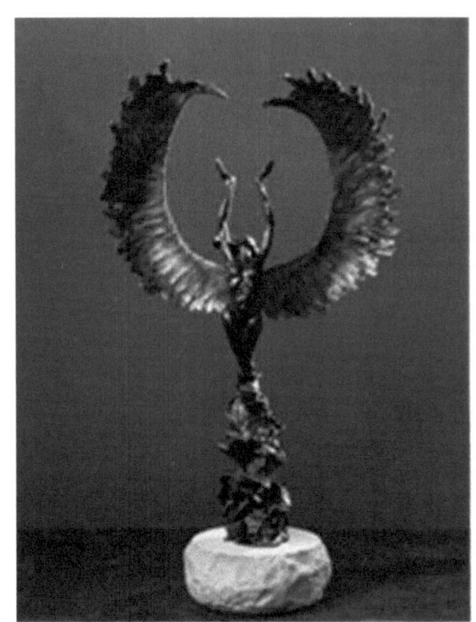

*Page 29 - 36*
*The Phoenix, 2023*
*Bronze*
*28 x 16 x 8 inches*

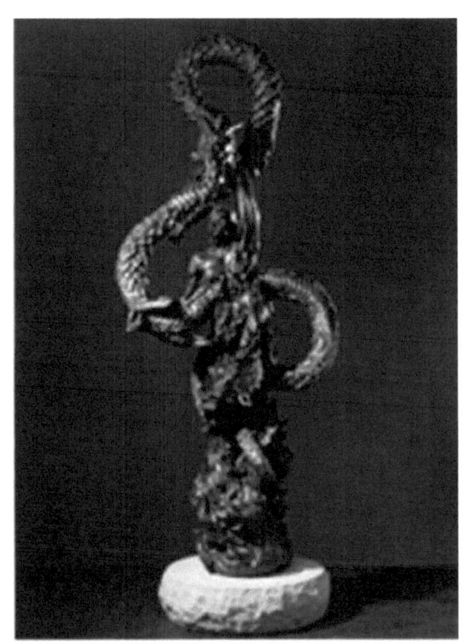

*Page 37 - 43*
*Leviathan,  2023*
*Bronze*
*39 x 17 x 12 inches*

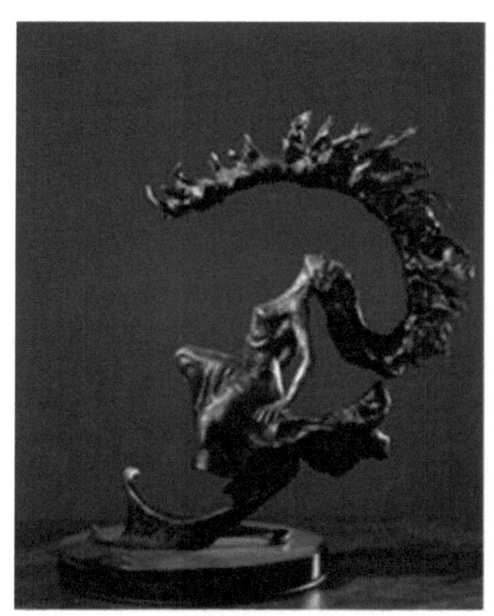

*Page 45 - 50*
*Sunset,  2020*
*Bronze*
*31 x 13 x 9 inches*

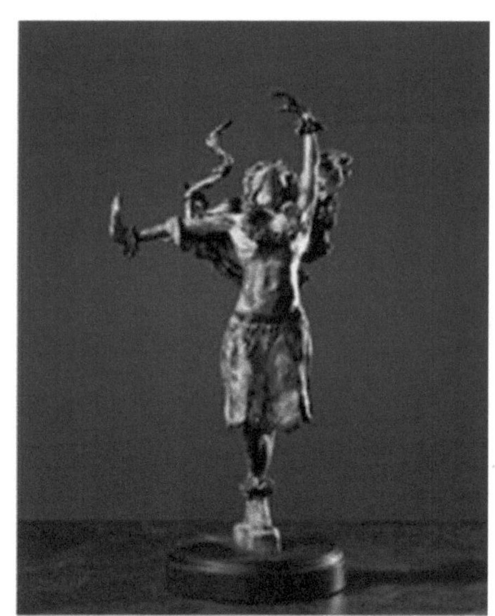

*Page 51 - 56*
*Storyteller, 2021*
*Bronze*
*23 x 12 x 10 inches*

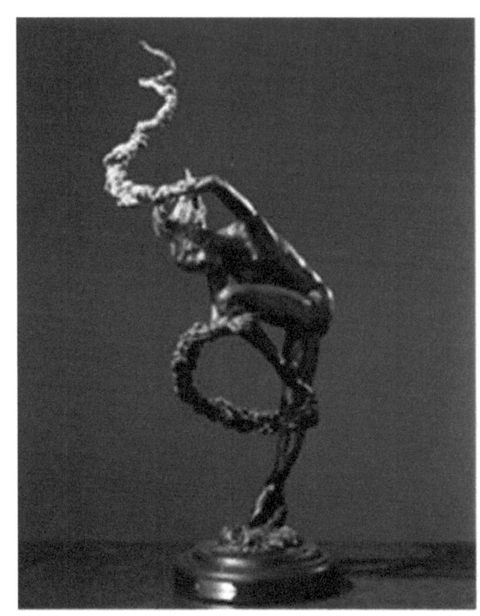

*Page 57 - 60*
*Eye of the Storm, 2020*
*Bronze*
*31 x 13 x 9 inches*

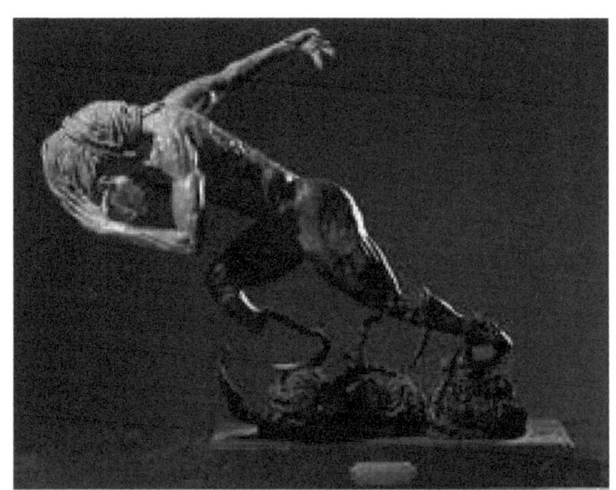

*Page 61 - 66*
*Rise, 2020*
*Bronze*
*19 x 22 x 9 inches*

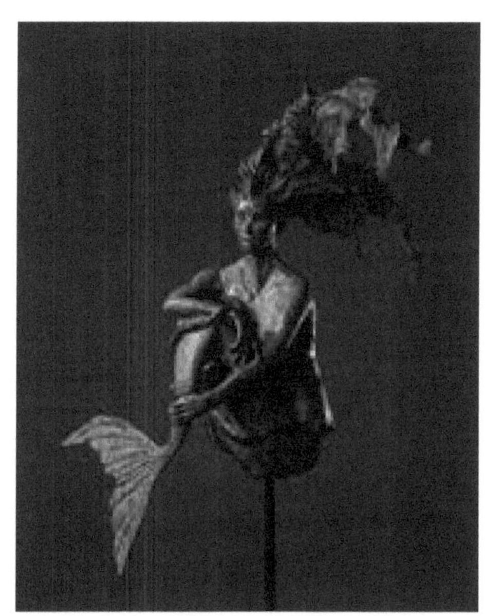

*Page 67 - 73*
*Hemeroscopium, 2022*
*Bronze*
*31 x 21 x 13 inches*

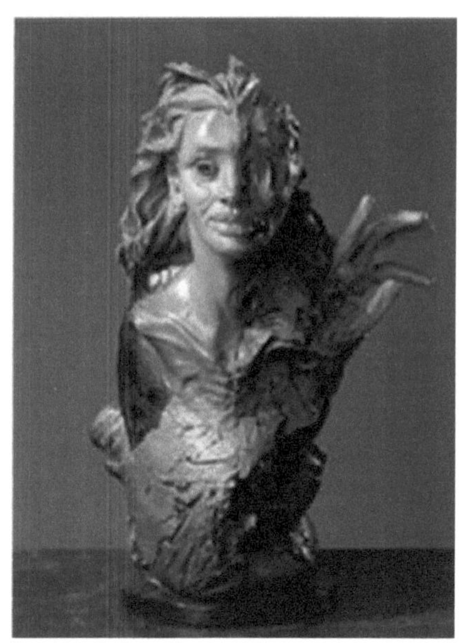

*Page 75 - 82*
*Refinement, 2022*
*Bronze*
*21 x 11 x 11 inches*

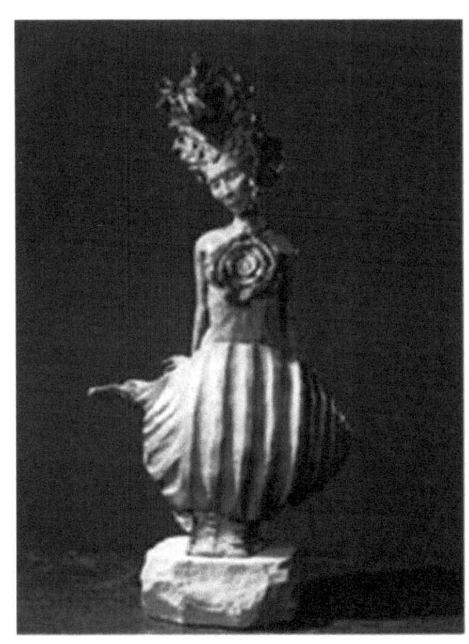

*Page 83 - 88*
***Birth of a Mermaid, 2023***
***Bronze***
*27 x 14 x 9 inches*

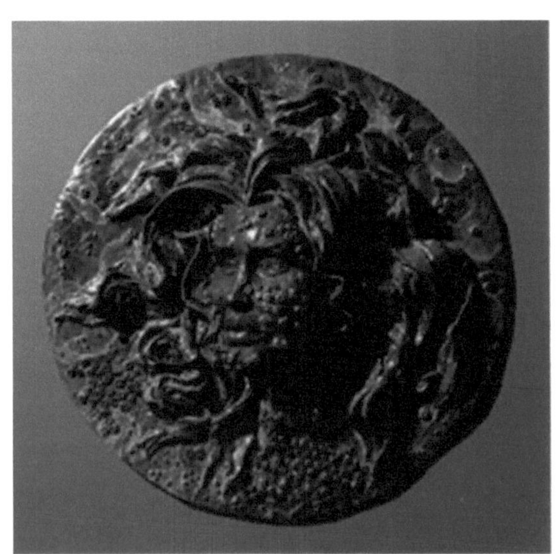

*Page 89 - 92*
***Ephemeral, 2023***
***Bronze***
*15 x 15 x 5 inches*

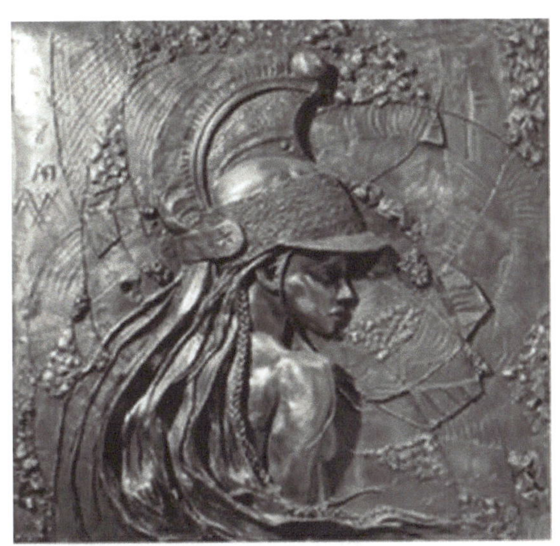

*Page 93 - 96*
*Sukha, 2022*
*Bronze*
*15 x 15 x 5 inches*

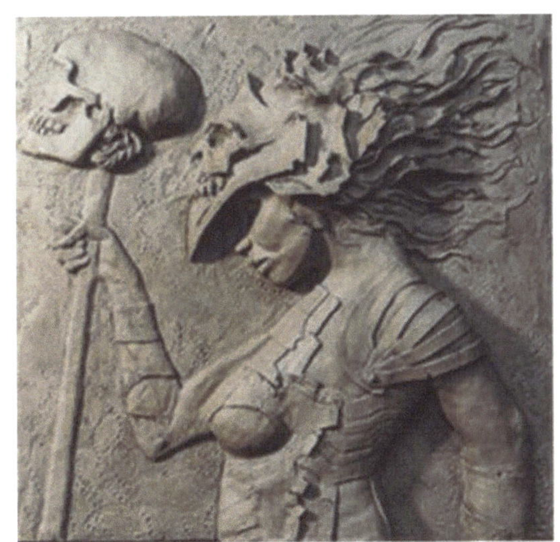

*Page 97 - 100*
*Dukkha, 2023*
*Bronze*
*24 x 24 x 5 inches*

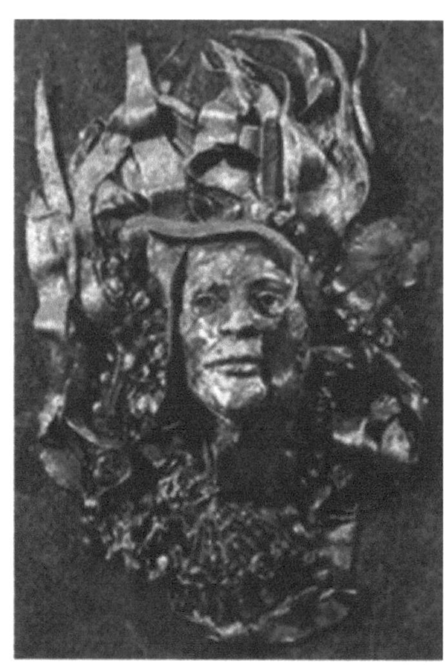

*Page 101 – 105*
*BlueMan of the Minch,  2023*
*Bronze*
*24 x 24 x 5 inches*

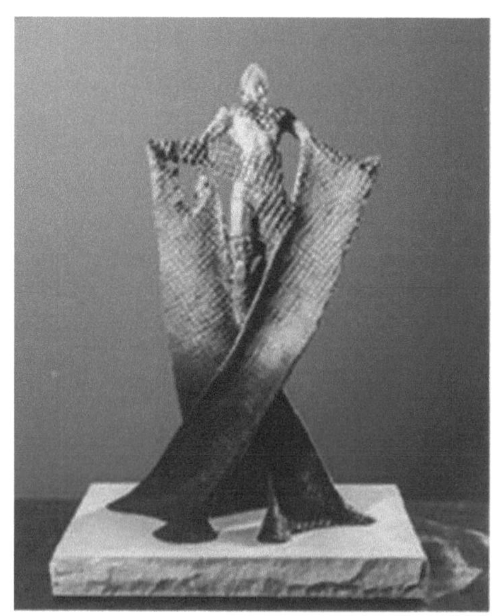

*Page 107 - 112*
*Freed by Forgiveness,  2023*
*Bronze*
*25 x 15 x 14 inches*

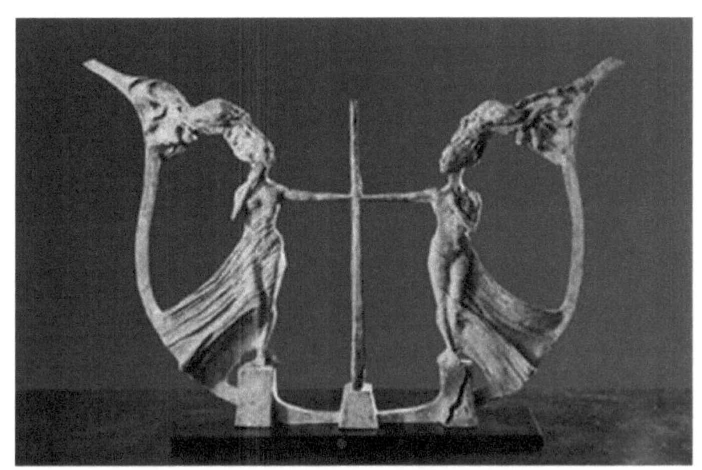

Page 113 - 118
Perception,  2023
Bronze
35 x 25 x 11 inches

9 781916 852709